A CHRONO

HISTORY OF BOLTON

FROM THE EARLIEST KNOWN RECORDS

TO 1876,

COMPILED FOR THE BOLTON CHRONICLE.

WITH

PARLIAMENTARY AND MUNICIPAI
REPRESENTATION.

BY JAMES CLEGG.

A CHRONOLOGICAL

History of Bolton.

A.D. 79 Roman Road from Manchester to Lancaster, by the Lane-ends, Hulton, Westhoughton, and Blackrod, formed about this time by Julius Agricola, after having reduced the native Brigantii ; another Roman road, from Manchester to Ribchester, passing through Cockey Moor. Whitaker, the historian of Manchester, fixes the ancient Roman station, Coccium, at Blackrod ; more recent historians, however, fix it at Ribchester. One of the eight forts erected by Agricola in Lancashire was at Blackrod

467 The renowned Arthur, King of the Britons, fought four of his successful battles against the Saxons upon the banks of the Douglas. According to tradition, the first battle fought near Blackrod was uncommonly bloody, and the Douglas was crimsoned with blood to Wigan

579 Smithills Hall, a royal Saxon palace, occupied by Ella, King of the Deiri, and subsequently by many noble families

580 Smithills walled round to keep the wolves at bay

606 Great famine in Lancashire

793 Eanbald, Archbishop of York, and Ethelbert, Bishop of Hexham, consecrated the Chapel of the Blessed Virgin at Smithills

1066 The Hulton family settled at Hulton about the time of the Conquest, and have remained uninterrupted lords ever since

1067 Roger de Poictou first lord of the manor of Bolton, receiving the manor from his cousin, William the Conqueror, who advanced him to the title of the Earl of Lancaster

1074 Bradshaw Hall erected. The family of Bradshaw were of Saxon origin, and were seated in this township before the Conquest ; after which event, Sir John Bradshaw was repossessed of his estate by the Conqueror, and passed to his posterity for 22 descents, whereof 11 were lineally knighted. The wife of one of these was Mabel, in memory of whom Mab's Cross at Wigan was erected, she having been obliged to walk barefoot and barelegged once a week from Haigh to the site of this cross, to expiate the sin of marrying again in her husband's absence when she thought he was slain. Her husband Sir William had been ten years away in the holy wars, during which time she married a Welsh knight, whom Sir William slew on his return

1100 Manor of Bolton passes into the hands of Roger de Mercheya, Roger de Poictou having been banished England for taking part in a rebellion against Henry I. Roger de Mercheya subsequently sold the manor with other lands in Little Bolton,

Haulgh, Sharples, Tonge, Breightmet, and 14 or 15 other townships, to Randolph, Earl of Chester, for 40 marks of silver (£26. 13s. 4d.)

1101 Turton Tower erected and licence for its castellation granted

1194 The De Lacys lords of the manors of Bolton, Breightmet, and Bury

1150 Woollen cloth trade exists in Bolton

1220 The fire beacon on Rivington Pike, at an elevation of 1545ft. from the sea level, believed to have been erected about this time, if not earlier, by Randulph Blundeville, Earl of Chester, who owned Great and Little Bolton, with all the lands between the rivers Mersey and Ribble, and for the better protection thereof erected a range of beacons, of which Rivington was the most northerly

1232 Earl of Derby became lord of the manor

1241 Edmund de Lacy enjoyed free warren in Deane

1256 Bolton raised to a market town by charter of Henry III ; Johan. de Bolton resides at manor house on the banks of the Croal

1298 The religious house known as the hospital of St. John of Jerusalem, in England, exercised feudal rights in Farnworth

1301 Tournament at Turton Tower

1310 The Hultons of Farnworth Hall, a branch from the parent stock of Hulton, were settled in Farnworth ; the last of the family at Farnworth died towards the close of the sixteenth century

1311 Geoffrey de Worsley obtained the manor of Middle Hulton in exchange with Richard de Hulton ; and from the Worsleys it passed to Lord Chancellor Ellesmere, and thence to the present Ellesmere family

1322 The forest of Horwich, 16 miles in circumference, was guarded by three foresters, supported from land in Lostock, Rumworth, Heton-under-the-Forest, &c. Wild boars, bulls, and falcons, for the chase, the ring, and the falconry were bred in the woods of Horwich, which had likewise their aëries of eagles, herons, and hawks

1337 Flemish clothiers settle in Bolton. Wooden shoes (clogs) introduced by emigrant Flemish weavers. Jannock (bread made of oatmeal) introduced by the refugee Flemings. To induce these refugees to settle in England, it was promised "that their beds should be good, and their bedfellows better, seeing that the richest yeomen in England would not disdain to marry their daughters to them "

1338 Blackrod Church existed

1412 Bolton Parish Church supposed to have been erected, though on the demolition of the Old Church in 1866, evidences were discovered that a church of the Norman period, some 300 years earlier, must have existed on the same site. The Old Church was re-edified 1517, and about 1533 appears to have been in its greatest perfection

1422 Up to this time Sir George Stanley claimed a market

every week at Bolton on the Friday, and one fair every year on the eve of St. Margaret, of two days' duration (July 19 and 20)

1450 Deane Church believed to have been erected, though some years ago, during alterations, an iron hinge was found on a door with the date 1412 upon it, and as early as 1200 there was a burial ground and chapel here called St. Maryden (St. Mary's, Deane)

1465 The manor of Great Lever awarded to Sir Rauff Assheton, of Middleton, against the claim of Roger Lever, of Bolton, gentleman—

The award given by the court at Lancaster was however resisted by Roger Lever, who in these lawless times took with him one John Lever of Bolton, yeoman, "with many and divers other evell desposed personnes to a gret nowmber," many of whom had been outlawed, probably in the contests between the houses of York and Lancaster, and proceeded from Bolton to Lancaster, where they broke into the castle and carried off the record of the recovery. Of this outrage Sir Rauff Assheton complained to the King and to the two Houses of Parliament, but though a fresh record was ordained and execution awarded, Roger Lever, with his abettors, "ryotously, with force of armes, defensably in the forme of warre arrayed, that is to saie, with bowes, arowes, swerdes and bylles, and other defensable wapenes, contynuelly during the space of five yere and more," occupied the manor and alse "daily and nyhtly robbed the seid Sir Rauff, his tenaunts, and many othes the Kinges leiges, kynne and frendes to the said Sir Rauff, of theire owne propre goods and catalles, and with force entered in their lyveloti, and the same despoiled."

1483 Hall-i'th'-Wood built; seat of the Norresses, a knightly family who took a leading part in the Wars of the Roses. The manor of Breightmet (Bright Meadow) was one of the forfeited estates of "our Rebell" Sir Thomas St. Leger, and conferred upon Lord Stanley by Richard III.; Sir Thomas St. Leger, though he had married the Duchess of Exeter, sister to King Richard, not only lost his estates by attainder, but his life by the hand of the public executioner

1494 John Lever, a great woolstapler, resided at Bolton

1486 Little Bolton Manor House built. Market Cross erected of stone in Churchgate—

This cross, at which till the passing of the Act of Uniformity in 1662 the Lecturer preached, had for its base a flight of five circular steps, surmounted by the shaft bearing date 1486. In 1651 a gilt iron cross was set upon its summit. It was removed in 1786 ostensibly for the greater convenience of the market, which was held there till 1826. The fish market was held there till the Market Hall was opened in 1855

1500 Walmsley Church existed

1510 Cotton yarns spun at Horwich

1513 Sir E. Stanley raises bowmen at Bolton to fight at Flodden Field; and it was to the "Bolton lads" who thus distinguished themselves that the following inscription on the walls of the Parish Church in 1701 had reference—

> The bolt shot well, I ween,
> From arablast of yew tree green,
> (Many nobles prostrate lay)
> At glorious Flodden Field.

And the ballad of the time ran—

> With fellowes fearce and fresh for feight,
> Which Halton feilds did turne in foores,
> With lustie ladds liuer and light
> From Blackborne and Bolton in ye Moores.

1540 Leland in his Itinerary gives us this picture of the Bolton of the sixteenth century:—Bolton upon Moore, market, standeth most by cottons and course yorne. Divers villages in the Mores abowt Bolton do make cottons. Nother the site nor the ground abowte Bolton is so good as it is abowte Byrl. They burne at Bolton some canals, but more Se cole, of the wich the pittes be not far off. They burne turfe also." Another author, Blome, writing about a century later, describes Bolton as a "fair well-built town, with broad streets; hath a market on Mondays, which is very good for clothing and provisions, and is a place of great trade for fustians"

1553 Following the dissolution of the monasteries, Whalley Abbey was granted by Edward VI. to Richard Ashton of Darcy Lever, together with great part of the demesne; Ashton made the abbey his residence. Muster of array from the Bolton gentry under Queen Mary

1555 Rev. George Marsh, vicar of Deane, burnt at the stake at Spittle-Boughton, near Chester, for his resistance to the Popish faith, April 24; the Bishop of Chester, in pronouncing the sentence upon him, saying "Now will I no more pray for thee than I will for a dog," to which Marsh answered that "notwithstanding he would pray for his lordship"—Tradition records that to this day the blood-red footprint of the martyr, deeply imprinted on stone, may be seen at Smithills Hall, the place where, having descended from his first night's imprisonment after being examined before Sir Roger Barton, and whilst on his road to Lathom to be further examined before the "council of blood" under the direction of the Popish Earl of Derby, he boldly called heaven to witness the righteousness of his preaching. Marsh was a native of the parish of Deane. It is recorded of him that he commenced life as a farmer, but after the death of his wife he "went to the University of Cambridge, where he studied and much increased in learning and godly virtues." As a minister he was noted for the earnestness with which he "set forth God's true religion, to the defacing of Antichrist's false doctrine, by his godly readings and sermons" in his native parish and elsewhere. In this year also, on July 1, John Bradford, a well-known preacher in this neighbourhood, was burnt by the Papists at Smithfield for advocating the reformed doctrines.

1560 Bradshaw Church consecrated

1563 Death of the Rev. Richard Rothwell, of Bolton, known as "Bold Rothwell, the Apostle of the North," and famed as an exorcist, who professed to have wonderful contests with demons. It was the boast of one of his descendants, a celebrated peruke maker in Bolton in the latter part of the 18th century, "I'm a real Rothwell; none of your Le'er-edge Rothwells, but a descendant of him that beat the devil."

1565 Horwich Chapel existed, the Commissioners for removing superstitious ornaments informing the Bishop of Chester that they had "taken away from Horwych Chappel, vestiment, albe, altar-cloth, corporasse, and other idolatrous gear." The old chapel was taken down in 1881, and the present church built on the site

1566 Rivington Church consecrated

1575 Death of James Pilkington, D.D., Bishop of Durham, Jan. 23; born at Rivington 1520; founded and endowed the Rivington Free Grammar School—
Tradition records that the twin piles of stones known as "The Two Lads" at Rivington were erected in memory of two of Bishop Pilkington's sons, who were lost in the snow on the hills; but there is no evidence to support the tradition except the coincidence that Bishop Pilkington had two sons, and that they both died young

1577 Death of Rev. Thomas Lever of Little Lever, chaplain to Edward VI

1587 Registers at Parish Church kept in Latin, the earliest known entry being dated January 21 in this year; this register was found several years ago beneath one of the stalls near the pulpit

1588 Preparations against the threatened Spanish invasion, watch towers and fire signals on Rivington Pike and other hills kept in readiness for months; Bolton, Manchester, and Middleton divisions being severally taxed for watching the beacon at Rivington

1590 Lostock Hall built by Christopher Anderton

1593 An entry in the Parish Church register records "Alexander Smythe, vicar of Bolton, buried in the church, the 28th day of December"

1594 Ralph Assheton, of Lever, high sheriff of the county

1597 February 5: First marriage in the Register of the Parish Church, James Crompton of Bolton and Dorothi Dudson of Deane

1602 Haulgh Hall built

1603 Witchcraft prevalent: several persons executed. Farnworth Hall built

1604 Hacken Hall, Darcy Lever, built

1609 July 14: Death of Martin Heton, D.D., Bishop of Ely, son of George Heton, of Heaton Hall, parish of Deane, aged 57—
It was to this prelate, on his refusal to comply with certain demands of her Majesty as to the temporalities of the bishopric, that Queen Elizabeth addressed the imperious letter—"Proud prelate, I understand you are backward in complying with your agreement; but I would have you to know that I, who made you what you are, can unmake you; and if you don't fulfil your agreement, by God! I will directly unfrock you. Yours, as you demean yourself, ELIZABETH." The original of this letter is said to be in the Registry of Ely. Heton, it seems, had promised the Queen to exchange some part of the land belonging to the see for an equivalent, and eventually he did so, but only after receiving the above letter

1610 Richard Bancroft, D.D., archbishop of Canterbury, son of John Bancroft, gentleman, of Farnworth, died November 2, aged 66. Bancroft, who was present at the death of Queen Elizabeth, was distinguished as an indexible opponent of Puritanism, so much so that Lord Clarendon, writing in his praise, says " If Bancroft had lived he would quickly have extinguished all that fire in England which had been kindled at Geneva." He took a prominent part in the famous conference of the prelates and the Presbyterian divines held at Hampton Court in 1604, when by desire of James I. he undertook the vindication of: the practices of confirmation, absolution, private baptism and lay excommunication ; and he was " the chief overseer " of the authorised version of the Bible, published within a year of his death. It was to Archbishop Bancroft that Lambeth Palace is indebted for the famous library which he founded and bequeathed to his successors for ever. He was buried at Lambeth

1619 In the Parish Church register are these entries : " Andrew Barton, of Smithalls, on the 14th of March was buried under the great chancel." "Christopher Anderton, of Lostock, gent., buried below the church, 12th November." According to tradition, these burials, as of other old families, were performed after dark by torchlight, attended with great pomp and an immense number of followers. It is also said that the interior of the church was illuminated. In this year eighteen noble and ancient families resided in Bolton and its neighbourhood

1620 Ralph Assheton, of Great Lever, created a baronet ; his son Ralph, also of Great Lever, elected M.P. for Clitheroe, 1640, and succeeded his father as a baronet, died 1680

1621 A grand banquet given in Lostock Hall to the gentry in this part

1623 Plague or sweating sickness in Bolton ; one-third of the inhabitants destroyed. Bolton parish contained only 2600 inhabitants, and Great and Little Bolton 500. The number of burials this year in the Parish Church yard was nearly 500 ; in 1808 the number was only 45. Parish Church Lectureship founded by Rev. James Gosnell (said to have been ejected from the Vicarage for nonconformity), who bequeathed for that purpose certain lands at Balderstone ; in 1691 it was further endowed from the Hulme Charity by the gift of eight acres of land on Bolton Moor

1624 Sir Rafe Asheton, Bart., of Lever, high sheriff of Lancashire

1626 Erection of St. Saviour's Church, Ringley

1628 Turton Tower and Manor sold to Humphrey Chetham, of Clayton, gentleman, and having continued in various branches of his family for more than two centuries, were sold some years ago to James Kay, Esq., in whose possession they still remain

1629 Dr. John Bridgeman, Bishop of Chester, purchased the manor of Great Lever from the Assheton family, re-built the Hall, and resided here during some part of the Rebellion. The Bishop's eldest son, Sir Orlando Bridgeman, chief baron of the exchequer, and afterwards lord keeper of the great seal, was the first Englishman advanced to the dignity of baronet by Charles II. after the Restoration, by the name of Sir Orlando Bridgeman of Great Lever

1631 Dr. Richard Pilkington, archdeacon of Leicester and rector of Hambleton in Bucks, died Sept. He belonged to the same family as Bishop Pilkington, and at the time of his funeral so dreadful a storm of wind, thunder, and lightning happened that the neighbours were forced to convey the corpse to the grave by lights at four in the afternoon. This occurrence caused the Papists, against whom he had preached and written, to spread several odd reports about him

1632 In the Parish Church register of burials we have this curious one under date 24th Sept.: "Yorkshire Dick, boy de Magna Bolton"

1633 Sixteen persons excommunicated by Dr. Syddall in the metropolitan visitation held at Bolton this year; they were denounced in the Parish Church on Dec. 7, 1634. Many of these were proceeded against in the ecclesiastical courts. These excommunications commenced 1632, and the catalogue ends 1737-8

1638 Bolton was at this time the principal market in the kingdom for fustians. Mr. Chetham, founder of the Manchester Blue Coat Hospital, was the principal buyer. When he had made his markets, says Aikin, "the remainder was purchased by Mr. Cooke, a much less honourable dealer, who took the advantage of calling the pieces what length he pleased and giving his own price"

1641 Bolton Free Grammar School founded by Robert Lever, citizen of London. Amongst other celebrated masters at this school have been Robert Ainsworth and Dr. Lempriere, authors of standard classical dictionaries, and the former of whom was moreover educated here. Dimities first manufactured in Bolton, this town then becoming a principal seat for the manufacture of fustians, vermilions, and dimities

1642 Civil war; Bolton, which was termed the "Geneva of Lancashire," and long considered the very school and centre of Puritanism, takes up the cause of Parliament, is fortified and garrisoned by the Parliamentary forces. Parish Church desecrated, and for two years used as a storehouse for military accoutrements

1643 February 25: Unsuccessful attack on Bolton by the forces of Charles I. March 28: Second unsuccessful attack on Bolton, the King's troops completely routed, and many of them slain. The Middleton club-men fought here, under Colonel Ashton, against the Royalist forces

1644 John Bradshaw, of Bradshaw, appointed by Cromwell, high sheriff of the county, which office he held for four successive years in contravention of the act of 1351, which created Lancashire a palatine county

1644 Prince Rupert's army of 10,000 horse and foot assembled on Deane Moor, previous to the storming and disastrous attack on Bolton, May 27. Siege of Bolton by Prince Rupert and Earl Derby, defeat of the Parliamentary troops and awful carnage among the populace, 800 or 1000 Parliamentarians and 600 Royalists slain, and the banks of the Croal strewn with their bodies, May 28—

According to one account, Prince Rupert refused to give quarter to the vanquished, and 1900 persons were put to the sword after the battle was won. Among the entries in the Parish Church register of burials for this year are the following: "13th Feb. A soldier buried from Thos. Coops." "17th Feb. John Rothwell, James Coops, John Greaves, Edmund English, soldiers; John Seddon, John Nuttall, Robert Dundy, yeomen, and 'six rebelles' were buried: killed 16th, buried 17th. All these were slayne in a very hotte skirmishe at Bolton, lasting four howers, that was on Thursday, February 16th, and the rebels of Wiggan were beaten backe in yt afternoon : they had shotten ther greyte cannen against Bolton fourteen times and yet were repulsed." "22nd Feb. John Buckley, a soldier." "9th March. A soldier from Roger Seddons." "10th. 23 of the Earle of Darbeyes men, all in one cave." And then following a long list of names, among which occur "Wm. Bootle, captain, and "Jo. Bradshaw, gent." we have "All these 78 of Bolton, slayne ye 28 of May, 1644." When the old Parish Church was taken down, a gravestone was found within the church to the memory of "William Gregg d. 1644, vicar for 14 years." Tradition says that this vicar was killed in one of the above attacks on the town

1644 Alexander Horrocks, a Puritan minister of considerable celebrity, was vicar of Deane at this time, and one of the Lancashire Committee of Presbyterian Ordination ; and was most probably the person referred to by Prince Rupert's troopers, when after "Bolton massacre," they exclaimed, "O, that we had that old rogue Horrocks that preaches in his grey cloake !"

1651 James seventh Earl of Derby beheaded at the Market Cross in Churchgate, Wednesday, Oct. 15, for his active support to the royal cause during the period of the civil war in which Charles I. was beheaded. As the unfortunate Earl's speech on the scaffold possesses an historic interest, we here reprint it from the work of the Rev. Canon Raines, "Memoirs of James seventh Earl of Derby"—

I am come, by the will of my Heavenly Father, to dye in this place, and I thank God I do, with all willingness and readiness, submitt to his most blessed will. Tis a place I desir'd to see when I was last in the country, both for the nutrall obligations that have bin betwixt this town and my family, as allso for your particular respects to me, whom I have understood to be ready to clear me from ye foul imputation, that I was a man of bloud, and that particularly I killed one Bootle here in cold bloud. I doubt not but there are here many men, present both that day this town was taken and divers other times during this warr, that can certifye I preserv'd many lives. But I know there is not any one present, that can lay the bloud of any man whatsoever to my charge, unless what might casually happen in the fury and heat of a battaile. And why I dye in this town I know not, unless it be to perswade the nation that I fall as a sacrifice for that bloud which some said I shed here, from which charge I am acquitted before you, and from which I had also cleared myself before my grand Judges at Westminster, had they pleased to hear me before they had destroyed me ; that report being hastily brought up among them by some, that I hope God hath forgiven, and too readily drunk in by others, whom I pray God to forgive. As for my crime (as some are pleased to turn it) which was objected against me by the Council of Warr, (for Bootle's death was never mentioned against me then, that being only secretly used to raise a prejudice against me in the judgments of such as did not know me)—my crime, I say, though I hope it deserves a far better name, was, that I came into my own countrey with my own lawfull King ; I came in obedience to his Majestie's call, whom, both by the laws of God and the laws of this land, I conceived myself obliged to obey, and according to the protestation I took in Parliament, in the time of that blessed Prince, his father ; so if it be my crime, I here confess it again before God, angels, and men, that I love Monarchy as the best government ; and I dye with love and honour ; and for the love and honour I bear to my master that now is, Charles II. of that name, whom I myself in this country proclaymed King ; the Lord bless and preserve him, and melt the harts of those that have power in this nation to accept him to his father's throne with honour and peace, for certainly, as I believe this nation will never be well contented, never thoroughly happy without a king ;

virtue, justice, great valour, and discretion far above so few years, doth now make him, in all places [where] he comes highly beloved and will hereafter make him honble. among all nations. And I wish ye people of this nation so much happyness (when my eyes are closed) that he may peaceably be received to the enjoyments of his just ryghts, and then they shall never want theyr just ryghts, which till then they will allways want. As for my being in arms in the beginning of this wary, I profess here, in the presence of my God, before whom within a few minutes I must make an account for this profession. I only fought for peace and setling the late King my master, in his just rights, and the maintenance of the lawes of this land, and that I had no other design, intent or purpose for my then taking up armes: and for this last ingagemt. I profess here again in the presence of the same God, that I did it for the restoring my lawfull Soveraign into that throne out of which his father was most unchristianly and barbarously taken; by the most unjust sentence of a pretended Court of Justice; and himself against law and all justice kept out and dispossessed of; and this was all my reason. For as for estate or quality I wanted not a sufficient competency; neither was I ever ambitious to inlarge either; for, by the favour of my King's predecessors my family was rais'd to a condition well known in this country, and now it is as well known that by his enemies I am adjudged to dye, and that by new and monstrous laws, as making me an enemy to my country, for fighting for my country—as a traytor to the laws for endeavouring to preserve the laws: but oh I God, give me grace to consider Him, who suffered such contradiction of sinners, and O my God, assist the King to his father's throne; assist the laws to theyr former honour; and restore Thy own religion in its purity, that all these shadows and fals pretences of religion may vanish away, and our children's posterities may serve Thee in spirit and in truth. Good friends, I dye for the King, the laws of the land, and the Protestant religion, maintayned in the Church of England, all of which I was ready to maintain with my life, so I cheerfully suffer for them in this wellcome death.

It is recorded that "at the words 'king and laws' a trooper said aloud, ' We will neither have king, lords, nor laws,' and upon a sudden the souldiers, being either surprised with fear at the strange noise that was heard, or els falling into mutiny, presently fell into a tumult, riding up and down the streets, cutting and slashing the people, some being killed and many wounded." His lordship interceded on behalf of the people, but his speech was again interrupted, and after the tumult was over he was executed

1653 The "toule of Bolton market is used to bee let for the yeare at 10s." Humphrey Chetham, a person of eminent loyalty to his soveraign, exemplary piety to God, charity towards the poor, and good affection to learning, died Sept. 20, aged 73, and was buried Oct. 12, at the Manchester Collegiate Church. He served as high sheriff of the county in 1635. He was the founder of the Chetham hospital or college at Manchester for the education, clothing, and maintenance of poor boys, whilst for the benefit of the poor of Turton he bequeathed the farm at "Goose Cote Hill," occupied for many years in later times as the Turton Workhouse. John Parker, of Entwisle, high sheriff of Lancashire

1654 An entry in the churchwardens' book of the Bolton Parish Church quaintly records, " Paid to sexton for whipping the dogs, 6s. 8d." St. Ann's Church, Turton, consecrated

1657 Banns of marriage published at Bolton Market Cross by the magistrates, who also during this period of the Commonwealth solemnised marriages in the Parish Church, The practice seems to have been to publish the banns "on three market days in three several weeks between the hours of eleven and two."

1659 October 31: Death of John Bradshaw, of Marple, sergeant-at-law, and president of the High Court of Justice on the trial of Charles I.; often confounded with his relative John Bradshaw, of Bradshaw Hall, near Bolton

1659 Sir Thomas Barton, of Smithills, died July 17, and was buried Aug. 17, in the choir of the Parish Church; and under an adjoining stone the remains of Sir Rowland Bellasis and Lady Ann his wife repose. Sir Rowland was buried from Smithills Aug. 16, 1699, by torchlight

1660 George Chetham, of Turton, high sheriff of Lancashire

1662 Wharton Presbyterian Church, Little Hulton, originated; Bradshaw Church re-built

1663 The Lecturer (then appointed by the ratepayers) preached at the Market Cross

1665 Death of John Bradshaw, of Bradshaw Hall; served the office of high sheriff of Lancashire 1644-7. The Bradshaws of Bradshaw were a branch of the family of the President

1673 Rev. John Lever vicar of Bolton to 1691

1684 John Okey, the celebrated Puritan, died; historic gravestone in Parish Church yard, bearing the following inscription—
John Okey the servant of God was borne in London 1608 Came into this Towne 1629 Maried Mary the daughter of James Crompton of Breightmet 1635 with whom he lived comfortably 20 yeares & begot 4 sonns & 6 daughters Since then he lived sole till the day of his death In his time were many Great Changes & terrible alterations 18 yeares civill wars in England besides many dreadfull sea fights The Crown or Command of England changed 8 times episcopacy laid aside 14 yeares London burnt by papists & more stately built againe Germany wasted 300 miles 200000 protestants murdered in Ireland by the papists This towne thrice stormed once taken & plundered He went thorow many troubles & divers conditions Found rest joy & happines only in holines the faith feare & loue of God in Jesus Christ He dyed the 29 of Ap & lieth here buried 1684 Come lord Jesus o come quickly

HOLINES IS MANS HAPPINES

Domine nos dirige.   Omnia sal sapit.

On this and two neighbouring gravestones are cut the armorial bearings of the Okey family

1684 December 16: Death of John Tildesley, M.A., vicar of Deane, and a native of Lancashire; one of the Presbyterian Committee of Ordination; a celebrated preacher and Nonconformist, thrice ejected, once imprisoned by Cromwell in the Tower, and afterwards residing at Manchester as a private individual, where he died aged 60. Vicar Tildesley married a near relative of Humphrey Chetham, and both he and his wife were buried beneath the venerable yew tree in Deane churchyard. Over their graves, placed side by side, still remain two small flat stones, bearing these inscriptions :—

<table>
<tr><td>Here lyeth the Body of
John Tilsley, Clarke,
Master of Arts, and sometimes
Vicar of Deane, which
was deceased the 16 day
of December 1684.</td><td>Margaret the Deare and
precious wife of John
Tilsley, Buried April 30th
1683, a most vertuous woman
in price far above rubies.
Prov. 31, 10.</td></tr>
</table>

1685 Death of the Rev. Richard Goodwin, M.A., aged 72. Mr. Goodwin was ordained by Bishop Bridgeman at Great Lever, and preached some time at Cockey Chapel. He became vicar of

Bolton in 1642 or 1644, the exact date being uncertain; but was expelled August 24, 1662, for nonconformity. He took out a licence in 1672 and preached twice every Lord's day at a private house in Bolton, where he died; he was succeeded in his meeting place by the Rev. John Lever. Mr. Goodwin was buried on Dec: 25 in the Parish Church. French refugee manufacturers from the Rhine settle in Bolton

1686 The manor of Smithills dependent on Sharples magna, the lord of which claimed according to prescriptive right a pair of gilt spurs annually, and the unlimited use of the cellars or wine vaults at Smithills for one week in each year; the last time this homage was exacted was in 1688

1690 Sir Charles Anderton, lay rector of Bolton, buried under the communion table in the chancel of the Parish Church. The Andertons had a right of burial there, and a marble stone was to have been laid over the tomb, but the then vicar and church-wardens refused to allow it, doubtless afraid that it would contain some Popish inscription

1695 Hulton Charity School founded and endowed by Nathaniel Hulton

1696 Bank-street Nonconformist (now Unitarian) Chapel erected

1702 May 4, death of the Rev. Oliver Heywood, a celebrated Nonconformist divine, who was born March, 1629, in Little Lever. Though ministering elsewhere, Mr. Heywood frequently conducted the services at the original Nonconformists' Chapel at the corner of Mealhouse-lane, Bolton (now occupied as a public-house, the "Old Woolpack"). He preached there on Sept. 18, 1672, soon after it was opened, and finally in June, 1696, when the congregation were about to remove to their new chapel in Bank-street, he administered the Lord's Supper to about five hundred communicants

1703 Death of the Rev. John Crompton, minister of "Cockey Chapel," Ainsworth, "a man of great worth and great humility."

1709 Death of James Cookerill, aged 106, occupier of the Man and Scythe when the Earl of Derby was executed. He was buried in the Parish Church yard on the 7th March. It is said that Cockerill suffered excessively in his family and fortune at the capture of Bolton by the Royalists in 1644

1714 Marsden Charity School in Churchgate founded by Thos. Marsden

1720 Sir Lawrence Anderton, Bart., of Lostock, sold his tithes in Eccles, Deane, &c.

1721 Died Peter Haddon, "a worthy, pious, learned man, vicar of Bolton 29 years, by whose death his friends had a loss, but the world a greater"

1725 December 31: Died, aged 56, William Baguley, of Oakenbottom and Kersley, gentleman, a man truly upright and pious; founder of a school for teaching poor children at Breightmet, of a similar one in Manchester, benefactor to the townships of Ringley, Outwood, &c.: he was buried in the Parish Church of Bolton. Wharton Presbyterian Church, Little Hulton, rebuilt

1726 Erection of All Saints' Church, popularly known as the "Chapel in the Fields"

1727 Epidemic in Westhoughton; one-third of the inhabitants swept off

1731 William Leigh, of Westhoughton, high sheriff of Lancashire

1732 Dec. 2: John Parkes, of Breightmet, high sheriff of the county. Dec. 23: Richard, afterwards Sir Richard Arkwright, born at Preston

1743 April 4: Death of "the learned Mr. Robert Ainsworth, 83 years of age, author of the celebrated Latin Dictionary"

1746 March 17: Court baron established for the recovery of small debts under 40s. in the manor of Bolton; court held every 21 days, and continued its sittings till July 8, 1776. The hearing costs were very moderate, being 6d. only; but the "increase" was as much as 16s. 3d. on a 30s. debt

1747 A Wesleyan Methodist society existed in Bolton

1748 August 28: John Wesley preached at the Market Cross, being his first recorded visit to Bolton

1750 Richard Arkwright carried on the business of a barber and peruke maker in Churchgate

1751 Wesleyan Methodist "preaching house" erected in Hotel-street

1752 Brindley erects his famous "water engine" to drain the Clifton Collieries

1753 Dec. 3: Samuel Crompton born at Firwood. "The Use and Importance of Early Industry. A Sermon Preach'd to a Society of Weavers and other Manufacturers, in the Parish Church of Bolton, on Wednesday, December 26, by Edward Whitehead, M.A., vicar of Bolton. Publish'd by the Request of the Audience"

1754 June 19-21: Bolton races; there was a single race each day, and "at nights assemblies for the ladies." October 26: Faculty for erecting a gallery at All Saints' Chapel. Duke's-alley Independent Chapel erected

1755 March 31: Richard Arkwright and Patience Holt married at the Parish Church. June 30: "It is agreed by most of the gentlemen of Bolton that there shall be no races, except they shall be such prizes as are according to Act of Parliament." October: Collection in Bolton Church for the Manchester Infirmary (established 1752), £9 15s. 6d.; Wringley (Ringley) Chapel ditto, £17 13s. 9d.

1756 August 8: Curious atmospheric phenomena at Hulton, in the parish of Deane. September 24: Died of a lingering fever, Mrs. Rothwell, wife of the Rev. Mr. Rothwell, of Bolton, and daughter of the late Vicar of that place: "A young lady that was not wanting in any of those virtues and graces which are the real ornaments to her sex, and which constitute a truly great and good character." Discovery of Roman urns at Crompton-fold. Cotton velvets first made by Jeremiah Clarke, of Bolton

1759 Duke of Bridgewater's Canal (Worsley to Manchester) commenced; first boat load of coals sailed over the Barton viaduct to Manchester, July 17, 1761. By the act for making this canal, the Duke was bound to sell his coals at Manchester and Salford "for no more than 4d. per hundred." On the execution of the works the price of coal in those towns fell to 3½d., or one half the former price. September: John Shaw charged with manslaughter at Spindle Point, near Bolton, was burnt in the hand, and ordered to remain in gaol three months.

1759: Died at Chowbent, in his 87th year, the Rev. Jas. Woods, a well-known Protestant Dissenter, commonly called General Woods, because of his taking the field at the head of his congregation to oppose the rebels in 1715

1763 Muslin and cotton quiltings first made by Joseph Shaw, of Bolton

1766 May: Death of the Rev. Mr. Rothwell, "the worthy Vicar of Deane, which living he enjoyed 56 years." Blackrod Church enlarged.

1767 James Hargreaves, a Blackburn weaver, invented a spinning jenny, by which he could spin from 16 to 30 threads at once, and without the use of rollers

1769 Richard Arkwright patented a spinning machine which he called the "water frame;" this machine carried a great many spindles, and formed the thread by rollers. Dorning Rasbotham, of Birch House, near Bolton, filled the office of high sheriff of Lancashire.

1771 Potatoes began to be grown at Bolton in the open fields

1772 Sept. 27: Died, aged 55, James Brindley, engineer of the Duke's Canal. At the Lent Assizes at Lancaster, Mary Hilton, for poisoning her husband at Middle Hulton, was ordered to be strangled and afterwards burnt.

1773 Population of Great Bolton 4568, Little Bolton 1036; total 5604; houses 1178.

1774 From a prize "merit" or ticket still extant, it is evident there was a Sunday School in existence in connection with the Parish Church so early as this time, though the date assigned to the foundation of Sunday Schools by Raikes is some nine years later, or 1783

1775 Invention of mule spinning frame by Samuel Crompton of Hall-i'th'-Wood, being a combination of the two discoveries,— the jenny by Hargreaves, and the water frame by Arkwright; its hybrid character, combining the jenny and the water frame, causing it to be designated the "Mule." Hy. Ashworth Esq., mentions that the "mule" is capable of spinning a pound of cotton to the length of 950 miles, or 2000 hanks, the "water frame" being capable of spinning a pound of cotton to the length of 19 miles, or 40 hanks

1776: Ridgway-gates Chapel built; John Wesley afterwards preached therein

1779 George, seventeenth Baron Willoughby of Parham, died at Rivington and was interred at Horwich Old Chapel, the barony becoming extinct. Machine-breaking riots, Samuel Crompton concealing his first mule in the attic of the Hall-i'th'-Wood, the rioters, according to a letter written by the famous Josiah Wedgewood, whose son was then at school in Bolton, announcing their intention to destroy all the engines not only in Lancashire but throughout all England. Bolton trotting originated about this time. St. Ann's Church, Turton, re-built

1780 Crompton generously gave his invention to the public. First spinning mill in Bolton erected in King-street by James Tweats or Thwaites

1782 Samuel Oldknow commenced manufacture of British muslins at Anderton

1783 August 22: The Bishop of Chester confirmed at the Parish Church of Bolton 1995 young persons

1785 June : Ridgway-gates Wesleyan Methodist Sunday School established ; on the first day there were only five scholars, but in less than 12 months there were above 500. On the repeal of the fustian tax in this year, silver cups were presented from Bolton, as the original seat of the fustian manufacture in the kingdom, to two Manchester gentlemen who had been conspicuous in their exertions to procure its repeal

1786 Removal of the Market Cross at which Earl Derby suffered. James Holland executed on Bolton Moor for croft-breaking. Sept. 13, having stolen 30 yards of cotton cloth, of the value of £3, from the bleach grounds of Mr. Thweat, of Burnden, cotton goods being then exposed on the grass for bleaching. In order that the most should be made of the impressive effect, the employers of the neighbourhood had their servants and workpeople assembled on the spot to witness the spectacle ; and on the following Sunday, the Rev. E. Whitehead, vicar of Bolton, improved the occasion by preaching a sermon upon the recent execution

1787 Thirty-three woollen manufacturers in Bolton, the woollen manufacture being the staple trade of the town

1789 William Hulton, Esq , of Hulton, high sheriff of Lancashire

1790 April 11: The Rev. Mr. Gilpin preached a sermon for Sunday Schools in the Parish Church, and there was collected £40 13s. 2½d. Little Lever Church consecrated. Steam engines introduced

1791 November 7: Death of Dorning Rasbotham, of Birch House, a well-known magistrate. December 25: New Version of Psalms first used at Bolton Old Church. Formation of Bolton and Manchester canal; its total fall from Bolton to Manchester, 187 feet. Population—Great Bolton 9000, Little Bolton 2000

1792 Act to enclose Bolton Moor and improve the town. Aug. 3: Sir Richard Arkwright, inventor of the water frame, and at one time a Bolton barber, whose shop was situate in Churchgate, died in his 60th year, leaving enormous wealth in land, money, mills and machinery. A young woman who had committed suicide buried in the highway on Manchester Road, about half-a-mile from the town, on Good Friday, a stake being driven through the body, as the jury had returned a verdict of *felo de se*. In 1824 some workmen who were digging a drain came across the coffin about four feet from the surface Steam engines first used in Bolton this year for the manufacture of cotton goods

1793 November 14: Death of the Rev. Jeremiah Gilpin, A.M., vicar of Bolton, aged 42. Unexampled prosperity of

Bolton muslin weavers, who brought home their work in top boots and ruffle shirts, carried a cane, and in some instances took a coach, weavers commonly walking about the streets at this time with a five pound Bank of England note spread out under their hat bands

1794 July 16: First stone of St. George's Church laid by Peter Ainsworth, Esq., of Halliwell. Bolton Volunteers raised; disbanded at the peace of Amiens in 1802; in 1803 a new regiment of 1020 volunteers raised under the command of Ralph Fletcher, Esq.; in 1808 they transferred their services with their colonel to the local militia, and served the country till 1815

1795 December 25: Organ first used at Bolton Parish Church

1796 Consecration of St. George's Church. Samuel Longworth gibbeted on Deane Moor for murdering in Deane-lane a youth of 18, named William Horrocks, a native of Westhoughton, and robbing him of his watch and four or five guineas; his body hung for two months on the gibbet, an object of terror to the neighbourhood, and after being cut down was buried on the spot

'1798 Hulton Charity School endowed. The Three Arrows public-house in Oldhall-street occupied as a workhouse from about this time to 1811

1800 " Squire K——," the famous impostor, trots the people of Bolton to the extent of many thousands of pounds

1801 William Callant, of Bolton, executed at Lancaster on the charge of having seduced a soldier from his allegiance. He was convicted on the evidence of a spy, by whom it was alleged he had been seduced into the commission of the act for which he suffered. It was openly declared by many respectable persons at the time that his execution was little better than murder, and it was afterwards generally believed that he was innocent of the crime imputed to him. Population : Great Bolton 12,549, Little Bolton 4867; total 17,416

1801 Under date June 24 the *Annual Register* records,—" A few days ago an entertainment was given by Mr. W. Smith, of Sunny Bank, near Bolton, to the descendants of his father and mother, who were within a convenient distance. Nine brothers and sisters and 210 nephews and nieces attended, making with himself (who is a bachelor) a company of 220 persons. After dinner the whole of this interesting assembly were seated on benches in regular order of descent with their numerous progeny, consisting of 71 persons, and the rest in succession, each separate family being collected together. This extraordinary sight was witnessed by a vast concourse of people, who were highly pleased with the scene, and generally struck with the respectable appearance of this family meeting. It is worthy notice, that in so extensive a family not one individual was prevented attending the meeting by sickness, although the typhus fever had for some time been prevalent where a great portion of its members reside"

1803 Pilkington-street Roman Catholic Chapel erected. Bridge-street Wesleyan Chapel erected. Bolton Light Horse Volunteers raised wholly from the gentry ; disbanded in 1818. About this time Robert Tannahill, whom Mr. French describes as "one of Scotland's sweetest song writers" (author of " Jessie, the flower of Dunblane," &c.), was a weaver of cambric muslins in Bolton.   Samuel Crompton at this time rented part of a factory from Joseph Wood & Co., employing three men, one woman, and six children.

1804 March 1: Death of John Horrocks, M.P. for Preston. Mr. Horrocks, who became one of the most noted and extensive manufacturers of his day, was the son of humble parents at Edgworth, near Bolton, where he was born Nov. 4, 1766, and was one of 18 children; his father, John Horrocks, being a member of the Society of Friends.   Young Horrocks was early put to work in a small factory at Edgworth, known as "Thomasson's engine," the proprietor of which, discovering accidentally the lad's aptitude for figures by noticing a sum in arithmetic which he had worked in chalk on the mill floor, generously sent him to school in Edgworth, and then one morning, putting him on horseback with himself, took him to a more advanced school in Shudehill, Manchester, where he remained until his benefactor's somewhat unexpected death.   The lad then returned home, his father having now become the tenant of some stone quarries in Edgworth, hitherto worked by the owner of the mill.   These quarries were famous for the "printing tables" they produced—not gravestones, as some biographers have recorded—these stone slabs being much in vogue then as a solid basement for stamping cloth with figured patterns.   Young Horrocks assisted his father in the management of this business; and very soon noticing that the cotton manufacture was rising into importance, and the spinning of yarn was done piecemeal —carding in one place, roving in another, and spinning in a third—he determined to start a carding engine of his own, which he worked by means of a water wheel at the old "stone mill" in Edgworth, which the Horrockses had hitherto used for grinding the stones smooth for their printing tables   Here cotton roving and spinning were soon added to the carding; and having thus commenced manufacturing in a small way in his native village, young Horrocks carried his yarn in baskets across his shoulder to Preston, a distance of 18 miles, sometimes walking it over the hills in clogs.   After a time he found that it would be easier to spin the yarn at the place where he sold it and he accordingly removed to Preston and commenced spinning there at the age of 21.   His enterprise was such that several individuals of capital who joined him became absolutely frightened at his boldness.   When trade was bad, and the manufacturers of Manchester, Bolton, Blackburn, and Preston were holding their goods in stock, he found his way to London, established a weekly auction, and there succeeded in disposing of his cloth at a handsome profit,—a circumstance long unknown to the Lancashire manufacturers, who had been predicting that by and by young Horrocks would break, and then the trade would go on as usual.   From that time he built factories one after another, and founded the well-known firm of Horrocks, Miller, and Co.   In 1796 he was elected M.P. for Preston, having then become so powerful as to defeat Lord Stanley.   He died at the early age of 37, leaving to his two sons a fortune equal to £15,000.

1804 Destructive thunderstorm, May 4.   "At Bolton and its vicinity," says the *Annual Register,* "the people experienced a most dreadful tornado, and it is supposed that a waterspout must have burst, the river Irwell having swelled to so great an height as to sweep away many buildings and large quantities of household furniture. At Hulton Park a ball of fire fell with such force as to split in shivers and tear up an ash tree, which had long been admired for its strength and beauty. Several bridges were thrown down"

1807 Mawdsley-street Independent Chapel erected

1808 Disturbances in manufacturing districts; weavers' turn-out in Bolton—Flash fight

1810 William Hulton, Esq., of Hulton Park, high sheriff of the county

1811 February 5: Rev. Thomas Bancroft, vicar of Bolton, died, aged 55. Erection of Fletcher-street Workhouse. Population 24,149—Great Bolton 17,070, Little Bolton 7079

1812 Great distress, rioting and breaking of machinery and political discontent in the manufacturing districts, Bolton being conspicuously distinguished among the disaffected places,—a petition from this town to the House of Commons, couched in extremely strong language, setting forth that the petitioners were in a state of starvation caused by destruction of trade resulting from the war with France, which they attributed solely to the misrepresentation of the people in Parliament. An extensive system of seditious affiliation, held together by secret oaths, was alleged to have been discovered by a Government spy. It was reported to the Secret Committee of the House of Lords that at a meeting of delegates in Bolton from several places it was resolved that Westhoughton Factory, belonging to Messrs. Wroe and Duncough, should be destroyed, and a troop of horse was sent to protect it, but the assailants dispersed before their arrival. Whilst the soldiers, however, were on their way back to Bolton the Luddites re-assembled and the mill was burnt down April 24, because of "weaving by steam." Three men and a boy were executed for the offence—Job Fletcher, aged 34, of Atherton; Thomas Kerfoot, 26, of Westhoughton, James Smith, 31,—and the boy, 14 years of age, named Abraham Charlton; they were tried at a special assize at Lancaster, and hung there June 13. A cart was sent from West-houghton for their remains, in order that they might have "Christian burial" amongst their own kindred; but it had to return without them. June 24: Parliament voted Samuel Crompton £5000 for his invention of the mule. It would probably have been £20,000 but that Mr. Perceval, Chancellor of the Exchequer, was shot in the lobby of the House of Commons by the assassin Bellingham on the very night—the 11th May—that the Chancellor had announced his intention to propose this sum. Crompton was at the time within a few yards of the spot

1812. Feb. Presentation of gold snuff-boxes to W. Hulton, Esq., and the Rev. W. Hampson, magistrates of the district to William Balshaw, Esq., boroughreeve of the town, and to Major Bullen, of the Royal Scots Greys, and Major Pilkington, commandant of the Bolton Light Horse Volunteers, from inhabitants of Bolton and its vicinity, as a memorial of public gratitude for their prompt and judicious exertions during the late disturbances in the manufacturing districts "in suppressing the riotous proceedings of misled and ignorant people;" also a silver vase to Ralph Fletcher, Esq., in testimony of the "gratitude of his townsmen and neighbours for his manly, loyal, and unwearied exertions in times of public commotion," and in approbation of his conduct as "a magistrate, a soldier, and a real lover of his country." "The friends of freedom in Bolton and its vicinity" on the other hand presented a silver vase and two silver cups of the value of 100 guineas to Dr. Robert Taylor, of Bolton, " for the spirit evinced by him in stepping forward to defend the character of the inhabitants from gross misrepresentation and for contributing to the successful exposure in Parliament of a detestable system of espionage"

1812 April 9: Destructive fire at the bleachworks of Messrs. R. Ainsworth and Co., Halliwell. Dec. 16: Died, in the 80th year of his age, William Orrell, clerk of Little Bolton Chapel 30 years and of the parish of Great Bolton 24 years. He was described as "a pious and sincere Christian and a friendly honest man"

1813 June 4: One T. Standish, of Blackrod, assuming himself to be heir of the late Sir F. Standish, with numerous followers assembled at Duxbury Hall and took forcible possession, turning out the servants. They continued in the house some days, but were eventually ejected by two of the Bolton magistrates, R. Fletcher and J. Watkins, at the head of a party of light horse. July: Killed "in the late splendid victory of Roncesvalles, in Spain, Lieut. Knowles, of the 7th Fusiliers, son of Mr. Knowles, near Bolton; was on two former occasions among the wounded." August 9: Died, in the 57th year of his age, the Rev. Joseph Bealey, minister of the Protestant Dissenters' Chapel at Cookey Moor; during the funeral sermon on the 22nd Aug., at which a very great number of persons were assembled in the chapel, the gallery being overloaded gave way; but being observed in time, fortunately all escaped without injury.

1814 June 7: Bolton Dispensary opened

1815 Rejoicings in commemoration of Waterloo. Napoleon shot and burnt in effigy .

1817 Second Improvement Act obtained for Great Bolton. June 11: Bursting of a lodge at Kershaw's Factory, Walmsley. Being in the night time, Mr. Kershaw, his wife, and nine children, who lived in a house adjoining the mill, had a narrow escape from death; factory and house destroyed. Oct. 22: Rev. R. Latham, vicar of Deane, died suddenly in the road as he was returning home from his duties

1818 Feb. 11: Bolton Gas Company established. March 7: Bolton Savings Bank established. Ormrod's first cotton mill destroyed by fire, July 20; numerous spectators seriously hurt by a falling wall; believed to have been set on fire by an incendiary. Pillory continued in use till about this time. This ancient instrument of punishment was erected at the parish pump on the site of the old Market Cross in Churchgate. Offenders thus exposed were frequently pelted with rotten eggs. " Rogues and vagabonds" were tied to cart tails and whipped out of the town by the bellman. In 1817 a man was pilloried here and flogged by the bellman, and in 1818 a woman was exposed in the pillory. It was not till 1837 that the pillory was legally abolished

1819 May 1: Streets of Bolton first lighted with gas. August 16: Peterloo. Nov. 19: Parish Church School opened. John Heyes, the bellman, imprisoned for announcing that Tom

Paine's bones had been brought by Cobbett to Liverpool. Duke of Lancaster's Own Yeomanry Cavalry raised. Fletcher-street Wesleyan Chapel built

1820 Bequests of large sums of money to various charitable institutions in the town by John Popplewell, a gentleman of the medical profession and a native of the parish, who died the same year. The bequests of this benefactor amounted to £15,099. His sisters Anne and Rebecca, who died in 1831, left £12,600 for similar benevolent purposes

1821 Discovery of ancient armour in Haulgh. Population of Great and Little Bolton 31,295

1822 Baptist Chapel (Moor-lane) built. Newport-street Primitive Methodist Chapel erected

1823 : Independent Methodist Chapel opened. General turn-out of factory operatives—turnouts billeted at other people's houses. July 5 : *Bolton Express* established

1824 According to Brown, who about this time published an incomplete history of Bolton, "The accession of new inhabitants and new dwelling-houses in 1824 was greater than during the long interval between 1587 and 1718." June 17th : First local Waterworks Bill obtained royal assent. September 29 : Sadler ascended in a balloon from the Bolton Gas Works and killed in his descent at Church-bank, Whalley. Oct. 9 : *Bolton Chronicle* established

1825 July 1 : Bolton Mechanics' Institution founded. Oct. 27 : Great Fire at Messrs. Hardcastle's bleachworks, damage £30,000. Nov. 1 : James Ormrod, Esq., of Chamber Hall, founder of the eminent cotton spinning firm of Messrs. Ormrod and Hardcastle, died, aged 56 years

1826 New Market Square and Little Bolton Town Hall opened. Great distress and serious riots in the manufacturing districts, the hostility of the rioters being directed against the power-looms, hundreds of which were broken in various parts of the county. Salford hundred had to pay compensation to the amount of £4,457, nearly half of which was for damage at one mill at Tottington, where 100 looms were destroyed. Bolton was, however, conspicuous for its orderly spirit; and on May 1, the King sends £500 to this town, in consideration of the distress prevailing here, "and the patience with which the unemployed poor of this districthad borne their sufferings." The local subscription reached £1,200, and £1,000 was contributed by the Committee in London. Over 170 loads of meal were distributed weekly among upwards of 1480 families. The master manufacturers and hand-loom weavers of Bolton united in memoralising Government in favour of a law to equalise wages, the masters' petition setting forth that a great proportion of the misery and distress arose from "uncalled-for continual reductions of the weavers' wages, attributable alone to men who, with few exceptions, had commenced the manufacturing business without any money, and with as little regard to moral right and wrong." The poor-rate levied in Great Bolton between April, 1826, and June, 1827, amounted to 16s. in the pound. At this time Bolton had only three night watchmen. July 25 : Death of the Rev.

John Holland, in the 60th year of his age, for 31 years minister
at Bank-street Unitarian Chapel. August 30 and September 11:
Green, the famous aeronaut, ascended in his balloon from
Bolton. September 11: Trinity Church consecrated. October
22: Death of George Blair, Esq., of Mill Hill, the well-known
bleacher, aged 60 years. December 18: The parochial chapel of
Farnworth robbed of its communion plate

1827 June 26: Samuel Crompton, inventor of the mule, died
in his house in King-street, Great Bolton, aged 74 years, " of no
particular complaint," but, in the language of his biographer
Mr. French, " by the gradual decay of nature, increased if not
hastened by a life brimfull of corrosive cares and mental
sorrows." July 6: Boiler explosion at Kearsley's factory,
Tyldesley, eleven persons killed and many injured. September 12: Died, aged 54 years, Dr. Robert Taylor,
of Bolton, who for many years took a very active
part in the exciting events of his time. A contemporary
notice says—" To the poor he was a constant benefactor, to the
world a friend, and to oppression and inhumanity of every sort
an unyielding enemy. He broke down the system of espionage
in England, by which he saved the lives of many, and thus obtained an enviable distinction in the judgment of his country."
September 23: Died, in his 80th year. William Lomas, who had
rung the treble bell at the Parish Church for the long period
of 75 years. October 27: Death of M. C. Dawes, Esq., of
Newport House, aged 54 years, an extensive local brewer,
through whose instrumentality the mails commenced running
through Bolton, a circumstance deemed of some importance in
the pre-railway period

1828 June 28: Bolton Express ceased. July 29: Death of a
centenarian at Farnworth, Margaret Tong, aged 102. August
1: Bolton and Leigh Railway opened, Friday, in the presence of 40,000 to 50,000 people; Mrs. Hulton naming the engine
that drew the first train. " The Lancashire Witch." Utility of
the line so strikingly manifested that in the very next week after
the opening there was a reduction of more than 2s. per ton on
coal in Bolton and the neighbourhood, and it was calculated
that the saving in fuel to the manufacturing population of
Bolton would be as great a relief to them as if all the assessed
taxes had been repealed. Died, August 3, aged 83, Ralph Ward,
apparitor at the Parish Church for 5 years. Bolton Savings
Bank at this time allowed 4 per cent. interest on deposits.
October 6: Public breakfast at the Commercial Hotel by the
Boroughreeve and the gentry of Bolton to the Home Secretary,
Mr. (afterwards Sir Robert) Peel, who during his stay at Hulton
Hall, as the guest of William Hulton, Esq., planted an English
oak, and in Bolton went through the foundry of Messrs. Rothwell, Hick & Co. Nov. 26: Death of Major Pilkington, of Silver-
well House, a leading local merchant and manufacturer

1829 Bolton Exchange opened. Old Mill Hill Factory burnt
down; one of the military killed while guarding the ruins.
This mill was at one time owned by the first Sir Robert Peel,
who was the first user of cylinders for carding cotton. April
13: Grand bazaar at the Parish Church Schools, for the
benefit of the Bolton Dispensary; net proceeds available for the
charity, £722 10s. June 10: The body of a man found sewn up
in a sack in Rose-hill tunnel, supposed to have been placed

there by the Resurrectionists, at that time very active in Bolton and the neighbourhood

1830 Trustees' Improvement Act obtained for Little Bolton. Foundation stone of Horwich Church laid May 21, on the site of the old chapel. August 12: Grand dinner at the Little Bolton Town Hall, to celebrate the recent Revolution in France; "Orator Hunt" present

1831 January 1: Opening of the Bolton and Kenyon Railway for goods traffic; for passengers June 13. Population of Great and Little Bolton 41,195. Feb. 13: Death of Mr. Thos. Beswick, aged 31, proprietor of the *Bolton Literary Journal*, and an extensive contributor to the periodical literature of the day. Feb 25: Witton Thomas, organist of Old Church, died suddenly. March 14: Ashton Worrall, 25, and William Worrall, 38, executed at Lancaster for the murder of Sarah McLennan at Failsworth, on Dec. 22, 1830. Deceased, who was 54 years of age, was the wife of a labouring man residing in Bolton, and was going to visit her daughter at Oldham, when she was waylaid and brutally outraged and murdered in a field adjoining the highway from Manchester to Oldham. July 20: Formation of the first Temperance Society in Bolton; the Rev J. Slade, vicar of Bolton, who presided over the meeting held in the Parish Church Sunday School at which it was formed, becoming its first president, and the Rev. John Jenkins, incumbent of Holy Trinity, its first secretary. July 23: Engineer and fireman of a goods train on the Bolton and Kenyon Railway killed by the upsetting of the engine

1832 Feb. 22: Ralph Fletcher, Esq., of The Hollins, for many years one of the most active magistrates of the Bolton bench and lieutenant-colonel of the Bolton local militia, died, aged 74. Enfranchisement of Bolton under the Reform Bill. Dec. 12-13: First Parliamentary election—Lieut.-Col. Torrens L 627 votes, William Bolling C 492, John Ashton Yates L 482, W. Eagle R 107; 1040 registered; 935 voted

1833 Jan. 15: Death of Isaac Dobson, Esq., aged 66, founder of the eminent machine making establishment of Messrs. Dobson and Barlow, one of the oldest of the kind in Europe. March 27: Presentation of a silver cup to Richard Oastler, the "Factory King," by the factory operatives of Bolton. March 27: Death of Richard Ainsworth, Esq., the eminent bleacher, of Moss Bark, Halliwell, in the 71st year of his age. December 31: Dreadful storm—chimney blown down at Messrs. James Barnes and Sons' mills, Farnworth, killing four young women in the weaving shed and injuring several others

1834 John Wilson, a private in the 35th Regiment of Foot, tried at the March assizes at Lancaster for the murder of Edmund Martin, a private in the same regiment, in the Barrack yard at Bolton on Oct. 4, 1833. The prisoner was confined in the guardhouse for being drunk, and while there he fired his piece among the men on parade, killing the deceased. He was convicted of manslaughter, and sentenced to transportation for life

1835 January 7-8: Second Parliamentary election — W. Bolling, C 638 votes, P. Ainsworth L 590, Robert Torrens L 343; 1020 registered, 927 voted. February 9: The notorious G. N. Silwood and three other prisoners escaped from the Little Bolton Starchamber, by burning a hole through the prison door. July 10: Ladyshore Colliery, Lever Bank, near Bolton, inundated by the bursting of the bed of the River Croal; seven men and ten boys drowned, 26 men escaping by the ladder pits. Nov. 19: *Bolton Free Press* established. Formation of Bolton British School. March 26: John Orrell executed for the murder of one of his children, by poisoning, at Bolton, the prisoner being strongly suspected also of poisoning another of his children and his wife

1836 Higher Bridge-street Primitive Methodist Chapel opened.

1837 February 4: Formation of Bolton Poor-law Union comprising 26 townships. July 26: Third Parliamentary election; P. Ainsworth L, 615 votes; W. Bolling C, 607; Andrew Knowles L, 532. 1340 registered; 1079 voted

1838 Death of the Rev. William Thistlethwayte, M.A., aged 62 years, incumbent of St. George's Church for 29 years. May 29: Bolton and Manchester Railway opened. June 24: Death of Thomas Rushton, Esq., the well-known solicitor, The Haight, aged 60 years. 25: Destruction of Royal George cotton mill by fire, several lives lost. Emmanuel Church erected. Oct. 11: Charter of Incorporation granted. Nov. 9: George Henderson, a young Scotchman, shot on Horwich Moor on his way to Belmont; murderer never discovered. 30: First election of Town Councillors: Dec. 1: First Mayor (C. J. Darbishire, Esq.) elected. In this year the first anti-corn law lecture under the auspices of the Anti-Corn Law Association was delivered in Manchester by Abraham Paulton, then a surgeon in Bolton

1839 Jan. 7: Terrific hurricane in Bolton, great destruction of property. Feb. 16: Death of Benjamin Dobson, Esq., aged 52 18: First bench of borough magistrates created. May 29: Court of Quarter Sessions granted. Jno. Gordon, Esq., appointed clerk of the peace, and John Taylor, Esq., borough coroner. July 3: Joshua Crook, Esq., founder of the firm of Crook and Sons, cotton spinners, died at White Bank, aged 61. Aug. 15: T. Hardcastle, Esq., of Firwood, the eminent bleacher, died. 16: Chartists went in procession to Parish Church and committed great excesses. Sept 21: Hiram Simpson, superintendent of the Bolton police force, shot himself at Liverpool. Nov. 5: Government police (about 40 in number) supersede those of the Corporation and Boroughreeves. 9: Robert Heywood, Esq., elected Mayor. Emmanuel Church consecrated. Great distress in the town; large numbers of persons unemployed; 1063 empty houses in Great Bolton in November, and one-eighth of the rateable value of property in the township untenanted

1840 Jan. 1: Temperance Hall opened. Elizabeth Lum built six almshouses at The Folds in Little Bolton for 12 widows or spinsters above 60 years of age, each of whom to receive a weekly allowance. Nov. 9: James Arrowsmith, Esq., elected mayor. St. Peter's Church, Halliwell, consecrated. Walmsley Church rebuilt

1841 July 4: Fourth Parliamentary election; P. Ainsworth L 669 votes; Dr. Bowring L 614; P. Rothwell C 536; W. Bolling C 441: 1442 registered; 1164 voted. Nov. 9: Thomas Cullen, Esq., elected mayor. Christ Church, Harwood, consecrated. St. Ann's Church, Turton, the second time re-built.

Great depression in trade in Bolton. According to a pamphlet published by Mr. H. Ashworth, out of 50 mills in Bolton, usually employing 8126 workpeople, 30 mills and 5061 workpeople were either standing idle or working only four days per week, the loss in wages being at the rate of over £200,000 per annum. Population of Great Bolton 33,603; Little Bolton 16,144; Bolton union, 97,519

1842 August 12: Charter of Incorporation confirmed. Great depression of trade; dearness of provisions; fearful increase of pauperism. Plug-drawing riots; provision shops plundered by mobs; 1300 unoccupied houses in Bolton; 10,000 persons receiving parochial relief. Sept. 9: Death of Benjamin Hick, Esq., the well-known ironfounder, aged 52. Nov. 1: First contested municipal election. Nov. 9: Robert Walsh, Esq., elected Mayor

1843 May 6: Betty Eccles the poisoner of her step-children at The Folds executed at Kirkdale. June 22: Bolton and Preston Railway opened. Nov. 9: Thomas Gregson, Esq., elected Mayor

1844 February 11: Matthew Ferguson, keeper of the menagerie at the Star Inn, killed by one of the leopards. July 2: Explosion at Brooks's mill, three persons killed. Christ Church consecrated. Sept. 1: James Horrocks, of Bradshaw Chapel, died, aged 100 years 5 months and 6 days; his father was born in 1677, and was 86 years old when his son James was born. Oct. 29: New Jerusalem Church, Bridge-street opened. Nov. 9: John Slater, Esq., elected Mayor by the casting vote of the retiring Mayor, Mr. Gregson, the numbers being 24 for Mr. Slater and 24 for Mr. Stephen Blair. At the same meeting, immediately after the election of six Conservative aldermen, the Council, by 22 votes against 19, dismissed the Town Clerk, James Winder, Esq., and by 22 votes against 10, elected as his successor James Kyrke Watkins, Esq. Nov. 30: St. Peter's Church, Halliwell, consecrated

1845 June: Lever Bridge Terra Cotta Church consecrated. November 10: First Conservative Mayor, Stephen Blair, Esq. December 15: Explosion at Rothwell and Kitts' mill, 14 lives lost

1846 Panic in the iron trade. St. Andrew's Presbyterian Church erected. Death of John Bolling, Esq., July 26, aged 56 years, cotton spinner, and for some years chairman of the Board of Guardians. Nov. 9: James Scowcroft, Esq., elected Mayor. December 15: Railway accident near Clifton Junction; driver and stoker killed and many passengers injured

1847 January 16: *Bolton Free Press* ceased. April 16: Bolton District County Court opened. May 27: Bolton Public Baths opened. June 5: Railway accident at Wolverton; amongst the killed was T. Makinson, a graduate of Oxford, and son of a Bolton tradesman. Improvement Act empowering Corporation to purchase Waterworks, &c. July 29: Fifth Parliamentary election: W. Bolling C. 714 votes; Dr. Bowring L. 659; John Brooks L. 645; 1531 registered, 1309 voted. Depression in the cotton trade; reduction of 10 per cent. wages. Nov. 9: T. R. Bridson, Esq., elected Mayor

1848 June 13: Bolton and Blackburn Railway opened. 22: St. Paul's Church, Halliwell, and St. Paul's, Astley Bridge,

consecrated.   August 30: Wm. Bolling, Esq., M.P., of Darcy
Lever Hall, died, aged 63; represented Bolton in Parliament
ten years.   September 12: Sixth Parliamentary election:
Stephen Blair O returned without opposition, Joseph Barker,
the Chartist candidate, having been withdrawn.   November 9:
T. L. Rushton, Esq, elected Mayor.   30: Liverpool and Bury
Railway opened.

1849 February 8 : Seventh Parliamentary election on Dr.
Bowring's appointment to the consulship of Canton. Sir
Joshua Walmsley R 621 votes ; T. R. Bridson O 568 ; 1437 registered ; 1189 voted.   27 : Peter Rothwell, Esq., of Sunning Hill,
the eminent ironfounder, died suddenly at Glasgow, in the 57th
year of his age ; public funeral at the Parish Church, Mar. 7.
June 30 : Royal Oak public-house, Churchgate, destroyed by
fire, George Radcliffe, a Breightmet man, sleeping there for the
night, was burnt to death.   Nov. 9 : T. L. Rushton, Esq., re-
elected Mayor. Dec. 19 : St. John's Church consecrated

1850 April 1 : Belmont Church consecrated.   June 18 : Loss
of the Orion steamship from Liverpool to Glasgow, on the rocks
near Portpatrick Light-house, about 10J passengers drowned.
including two from Bolton, Mr. William Latham, of Kay-street,
machine maker, and Mr. Robert Haslam, tripe dealer, Deansgate ; Mr. Jonathan Settle, of the One Horse Shoe, Market
Square, was in the vessel, but saved his life by swimming, and
was picked up by a boat. Amongst the drowned was Mr. Roby,
a Rochdale banker, author of "Traditions of Lancashire."
Nov. 1 : James Cross, Esq., the well known solicitor, died at
Halliwell Lodge, in the 30th year of his age.   9 : William Gray,
Esq., elected Mayor.

1851 Population of the borough, 61,172—Great Bolton 39,923:
Little Bolton 19,989 ; Haulgh 1362 ; Bolton union 114,168.
Edward Greenhalgh appointed master of the Bolton Workhouse.
July 11 : Wesley Chapel, Bradshawgate, opened.   Sept. 29 :
St. Michael's Church, Great Lever, consecrated.   Nov. 8 : Explosion at Great Lever Colliery, three lives lost ; two bodies not
recovered till Dec. 31.   Oct. 9-11 : Queen visits Worsley. 11 :
Prince Albert visits Bolton and Dean Mills, Halliwell.   Nov.
10 : W. Gray, Esq., re-elected Mayor.   21 : Earl of Shaftesbury
visited Bolton, and was presented with an address from the
factory operatives, acknowledging his advocacy of their cause
for 20 years.   Dec. 21 : First Ordination in the Bolton Parish
Church by Bishop of Manchester

1852 Jan. 10: Disputes in the iron trades, 10,353 hands on
strike in Bolton and Manchester district ; the strike lasted six
months and was accompanied by great distress.   Feb. 11 : The
Town Council, on the motion of Mr. Councillor James Greenhalgh, unanimously resolved to take steps for the adoption of the
Public Free Library and Museum Act in Bolton ; and on March
26, a poll of the burgesses resulted in the adoption of the Act, 862
voting for and only 55 against it.   July 8 : Eighth Parliamentary
election—Thomas Barnes L 745 votes, Joseph Crook L 727 ;
Stephen Blair O 717, Peter Ainsworth L 316 ; 1671 registered,
1579 voted.   13 : Destruction of Star Inn concert room by fire.
19 : Three persons killed by the falling of the Star Inn wall.
Aug. 23 : Railway accident at Bullfield, suicide of the points-
man.   Sept. 24: Opening of factory operatives' exhibition and
bazaar in commemoration of Ten Hours Bill.   Nov. 9: John Stones,

Esq., elected, Mayor. 14: Methodist New Connexion Chapel, St. George's Road, opened. Rain fell in Bolton 77 days consecutively (including 12 Sundays), terminating Dec. 25. Hurricane on Christmas morning. Season of unexampled prosperity; erection of mills; general improvement of the town

1853 March 4: Railway accident at Clifton Junction, six persons killed and upwards of 14 injured. July 29: Three persons suffocated by foul air in a well at Ballfield, two of them through their gallantry in attempting to rescue others. Oct. 12: Bolton Free Library opened. Strikes among the factory operatives for an advance of 10 per cent. Nov. 9: P. R. Arrowsmith, Esq., elected Mayor

1854 Jan. 1—5: Great snow storm, railways and highways blocked up by snowdrifts, traffic impeded, works stopped, in some instances the snow reaching to the bedroom windows of dwellings; on the 2nd, at 8 30 p.m., the thermometer stood at 26 degrees below the freezing point. 20: Lord Bradford set apart 20 acres of ground between Tong bridge and Lever bridge as public park. June 10: St. Saviour's Church, Ringley, consecrated after re-building. 19: Opening of the Industrial Ragged Schools, Commission-street. July 10: Improvement Act received Royal assent. Aug. 24: John Albinson, Esq., of Chapel-alley, the well-known antiquary, died, aged 79 years: his library consisted of 20,000 vols., including the celebrated Bowyer Bible (45 vols.), valued at 3,100 guineas, and in March, 1856, when the library was sold by auction, this Bible was purchased for £550 by Robert Heywood, Esq., of The Pike, in whose family it now remains. Nov. 9: P. R. Arrowsmith, Esq., re-elected Mayor.

1855 Severe frost from middle of January to beginning of March; great distress in the iron and cotton trades; soup kitchens established; 7000 hands unemployed. July 30: Opening of the Church Institute. November 1: Consecration of St. James's Church, Breightmet; 9: Jas. Knowles, Esq, elected Mayor; 19: Fire at Christ Church, organ destroyed. December 19: Market Hall opened

1856 April 21: Presentation of dress sword to Major Langshaw by the Bolton troop of the Duke of Lancaster's Own Yeomanry, with which he had been connected from its formation. July 9: Wellington Mills, Little Bolton, destroyed by fire. August 21: Bank-street Unitarian Chapel reopened (after being re-built). November 10: Partial destruction of Smithills Chapel by fire; James Knowles, Esq., re-elected Mayor. 17: Visit of Kossuth, the Hungarian patriot, to Bolton. Dec. 26: The Cemetery in Tonge opened. December 29: Rev. Canon Slade resigned the Vicarage of Bolton after nearly 40 years' ministration, retiring to his rectory at West Kirby

1857 January 19: Explosion of a locomotive boiler at Sough, on the Bolton and Blackburn line, killing Daniel Greenwood, the driver, and Henry Young, the guard, both of Bolton. February 7: Rev. Henry Powell inducted to the vicarage of Bolton. March 28: Ninth Parliamentary election, Captain Gray L C 990 votes; Joseph Crook L 805; Thomas Barnes L 833; 1933 on the register, 1678 voted. May 12: Post Office removed from Bradshawgate to Market Square. July 1: Mr John Fawcett, jun., Mus. Bac. Oxon., and organist of the Bolton Parish Church, died, aged 32; 15: Heaton Waterworks completed and water first turned on. November 9: William

Makant, Esq., elected Mayor. Dec. 7: Aaron Mellor sentenced to death at Liverpool Assizes, for the murder of his wife in Deansgate, Bolton; sentence subsequently commuted to penal servitude for life, because of a mistake in the swearing of a juror named Thorne instead of one Thornley. 28. Death of Mr. William Holt, aged 72, one of the most zealous supporters of the Conservative cause in Bolton. His brother Conservatives erected a handsome monument to his memory in the Cemetery. Commercial crisis; depression in the cotton and iron trades, November and December.

1858 January 23: Death of Mr. Matthew Butcher, aged 80 years, for many years inspector of weights and measures for the Bolton division of the county. 28: Destruction of Great Moor-street Railway Station by a luggage train, one man killed. June 14; John Gaskell, Esq., public prosecutor for this borough for 15 years, died aged 41; John Hall. Esq., appointed his successor June 17. Sept. 8: Corner stone of New Workhouse at Fishpool laid by James Winder, Esq., chairman of the Board of Guardians. Thos. Bonsor Crompton, Esq., the eminent paper manufacturer, and the last male representative of the Farnworth branch of the Cromptons, died in the 67th year of his age. 17: Rev. Henry Richardson, for nearly 40 years Lecturer of the Parish Church, died at Poulton-le-Fylde, aged 64. Oct. 28: Major Kearsley, when out hunting, had his horse killed by falling down a coal pit; he most miraculously escaped. Nov. 9: William Makant, Esq., re-elected Mayor. Dec. 10: Redistribution of Bolton Lectureship Charity sanctioned: Lecturer to have £150 per annum and Vicar not exceeding £100 in augmentation of his vicarage income to £350; surplus funds towards the creation of new ecclesiastical districts in the ancient parish. Theatre in Mawdsley-street converted into a Concert Hall.

1859 February 15: Opening of Concert Hall in Mawdsley-street. 10: Death of John Stones, Esq., Mayor of the borough 1852-3. March 28: Died at the Bolton Workhouse, Esther Holden, a native of Edgworth, aged 105 years. April 29: General election: Captain Gray (second time) and Joseph Crook (third time) returned; no opposition. June 10: First drinking fountain in Bolton erected near Swan Hotel. 30: St. John's Church, Wingates, consecrated. July 2: Visit of Historic Society of Lancashire and Cheshire to Bolton and Rivington; carriage accident on return journey from Rivington, and several gentlemen seriously injured. 14: Death of Thomas Cullen, Esq., aged 83 years, one of the magistrates for this borough, and Mayor in 1841-2. October 8: Death of Mr. Thomas Moscrop, of Back-o'-th'-Bank, aged 71 years, whose family had occupied the same house for the last 300 years, and he was the last survivor of that branch of the Moscrops—a family, which came into Lancashire with the Sutherlands of Ormskirk in 1513, when the battle of Flodden Field was fought. Nov. 9: John Orton, Esq., elected Mayor. Sunday, Nov. 13: Carlile No. 3 Mill, belonging to Messrs. Bolling, destroyed by fire. 15: Bolton (27th Lancashire) Rifle Volunteer Corps established. 18: Death of Mr. John Addle-shaw, of Wood-street, aged 57 years, senior agent of the British Temperance League. 30: Brook Mill, Deansgate, on the site of the old "Salt Pie Factory," destroyed by fire. Dec. 3: Death of Mr. John Thirlwind, of Bradshawgate, aged 79 years, for 40 years a member of the Society of Friends. He was never absent from Bolton a fortnight at one time during his long life. 5: Rev. James Dawson, incumbent of Belmont, died at Newton-in-Cartmel. 17: Opening of new offices of *The Bolton Chronicle* in Knowsley-street. 21. Death of Mr. James Lomax, of the firm of Lomax and Sons, the well-known auctioneers. Great revival services, conducted by Professor Finney, from America, commenced in Bolton this month.

1860 January: Great Wesleyan chapel building movement in the Bolton circuits. Feb. 29: Death of Mr. Samuel Hodgkinson, in his 65th year; a well-known member of the Society of Friends, and one of the representatives of Derby Ward in the Town Council. May: Bolton and Great Lever (18th Lanc.) Volunteer Artillery Corps established. 15: Death of Rev. Canon Slade at Crompton Fold, in the 78th year of his age. June: R. R. Rothwell, Esq., of Sharples Hall, created a Count of the Sardinian kingdom, by the title of Count (afterwards Marquess) De Rothwell. 26: Death of Mr. Thomas Kenyon, aged 76, for 31 years master of the Hulton Street School, one of the earliest Volunteers in the Bolton Local Militia, and 21 years librarian of the Mechanics' Institute. Aug. 21: Death of Edward Bolling, Esq., the well-known cotton spinner. September 12 and 13: Great Show in Bolton of the Manchester and Liverpool Agricultural Society. Oct. 16: Death of John Mawdsley, Esq., of Black Bank, over 42 years actuary of the Bolton Savings Bank. November 9: John Harwood Esq., elected Mayor. 29: Eugenie Empress of the French passed through Bolton. December 6: Heaviest rainfall of any day in this excessively wet year. Trade generally good throughout the year.

1861 January 24: Monument over Crompton's grave in Parish Churchyard. 31: J. Crook, Esq., resigned his seat in Parliament. February 9: Presentation to G. J French, Esq., of a writing desk made out of one of Crompton's mules. 11. Thomas Barnes (L) elected M.P. unopposed. March 14: 12,000 factory operatives on strike until 20th April against a reduction of five per cent. April 8: General turnout of powerloom weavers of South Lancashire. 8: Census of the borough taken; population of Great Bolton 43 435, Little Bolton 26,892, Haulgh 1069—total borough, 70,396; Bolton union 130,270.—May 30: Independent Oddfellows' A.M.C. in Bolton. 31: Fletcher-street new Wesleyan Chapel opened. August 1: Mr. Crook's Bleachers' Short Time Act came into operation. 3: Presentation of timepiece, worth 70 guineas, to Joseph Crook, Esq., late M.P. for Bolton, by the operative bleachers. 8: Opening of Holy Trinity Lever-street Schools. Sept. 26: Opening of New Workhouse at Fishpool. Nov. 9: J. R. Wolfenden, Esq., elected mayor. 21: Death of John Slater. Esq., of Back-o'-th'-Bank, aged 64 years, one of the borough magistrates and Mayor in 1844-5. 23: Peal of bells at Holy Trinity, presented by Dr. Chadwick. December: Great depression in cotton trade owing to civil war in United States. Trade generally du l

1862 February: Spread of the Co-operative movement. Feb. 23: Death of James Winder, Esq., solicitor, of Ainsworth House, in the 62nd year of his age, first Town Clerk of the borough, and clerk to the borough magistrates from the appointment of the first Bench in 1839; he was one of the leading promoters of the Charter of Incorporation. March 6: Robert

Winder, Esq., appointed clerk to the borough magistrates in succession to his late father. 15: Corner stone of St. Paul's Church, Deansgate, laid by the Bishop of Manchester. April 6: Opening new organ presented by Dr. Chadwick to the Workhouse. 18: Corner stone of Congregational Church, St. George's-road, laid. 23-25: Volunteer Bazaar in Temperance Hall, proceeds £2540. July: Rapid spread of distress and formation of relief committees throughout the manufacturing districts. August: Stoppage of many mills in Bolton from the scarcity of cotton. September 24: Statue of Samuel Crompton, inventor of the mule, inaugurated. The statue is erected on Nelson-square, and cost over £1900. Oct. 5: Opening of St. James's School Church, Waterloo. 6: Lord Palmerston directed a gratuity of £50 to John, only surviving son of Samuel Crompton. 12: Public meeting on the distress in the borough; £4000 subscribed. 23: Gift of a free recreation ground, Lever-street, Bolton-moor, by Robt. Heywood, Esq. November 10: J. R. Wolfenden, Esq., re-elected Mayor. December 2: Great county meeting at Manchester for relief of Lancashire distress—£130,000 subscribed. 6: Bolton special relief fund raised to £10,000. 16,647 persons relieved in the week by Relief Committee and Board of Guardians jointly

1863 January: Operatives out of employment in the borough, 6405. 24: Death of Thos. R. Bridson, Esq., Mayor of the borough 1847-8. March 4: Opening of Park-street Wesleyan Chapel. April 3: Opening of Congregational New Church, St. George's Road. May: Retirement of Dr. Chadwick from Bolton; public testimonials to himself and Mrs. Chadwick, including silver plate from the gentry. June 19: Consecration of Holy Trinity Church, Prestolee. July 11: Presentation at Southport to Dr. Chadwick of his full-length portrait, subscribed for by upwards of 7000 working men and women in Bolton; writing desk from the same to Mrs. Chadwick. August 25: Adoption of Local Government Act at Farnworth. October 6: Earthquake in Bolton. Formation of Working Men's Club in Bolton. November 1: John Ashton Yates, Esq., one of the Liberal candidates for the representation of Bolton at the first Parliamentary election in 1832, died at the Park, near Manchester, aged 68 years. 5: Adoption of Local Government Act at Halliwell. 10: Richard Harwood Esq., elected Mayor. 25: Opening of St. Paul's Church. December 1: Death of John Woodhouse, Esq., solicitor, clerk of the Bolton Union, aged 69 years; Mr. Simpson Cooper being elected as his successor on the 16th. 3: Violent storm and destruction of property. 5: Number in receipt of relief by guardians, 4835; by Relief Committee, 2360. Continuance of cotton famine, though distress decreasing

1864 Jan. 12: Opening of St. James's Church, New Bury. Death of Giles Cross, Esq., land surveyor, aged 70. 15: James Hudsmith, Esq., proprietor of The Bolton Chronicle, died in his 48th year. February 17: Election of first Local Government Board, Astley Bridge. 27: Working Men's Club opened, Bank House. March 30: Death of William Hulton, Esq., of Hulton, in the 77th year of his age; he was High Sheriff of the county in 1810. April 9: Retirement of the Rev. F. Baker, M.A., from the pastorate of Bank-street Chapel. June 3: Moses Holden, the celebrated astronomer, a native of Bolton, died at Preston, aged 87 years. July 4: Farnworth Park presented by Thomas Barnes, Esq., M.P. 25: Resignation of Jas.

Knowles, Esq., Town Clerk, which office he had held for more than 16 years. August 3: Explosion of naphtha still at the Gas Works, Moor-lane; four men killed and several injured. 9: Corner-stone of New Fish Market laid by the Mayor (Ald. Richard Harwood). 10: R. G. Hinnell, Esq., solicitor, elected Town Clerk of the borough. 24: Opening of the Tyldesley, Eccles, and Wigan Railway. 31: First show of Deane Agricultural Society. Oct. 11: The Right Hon. W. E. Gladstone, M.P., Chancellor of the Exchequer, visited Bolton. 12: Inauguration of the People's Park at Farnworth by the Chancellor of the Exchequer. Nov. 9: Richard Stockdale, Esq., elected Mayor. Dec. 19: John Musgrave, Esq., the venerable head of the firm of Messrs. Musgrave and Sons, Globe Iron-works, died at the age of 80 years.

1865 January 14: John Mangnall, Esq., of High Lawn, Sharples, died, aged 94, an alderman of the borough for nearly fourteen years. 21: Railway collision near Daubhill; three persons killed and eleven injured. February 2: Fire at the Higher Mill of T. Barnes, Esq., M.P., Dixon Green; damage, £5000. 7: Death of Thomas Gregson, Esq., at Southport, aged 70 years, one of the first aldermen of this borough, and mayor in 1843-4. March 23: Death of the Right Hon. the Earl of Bradford, at Weston Park, Salop, aged 75. 24: Presentation of portrait to Ald. Richard Harwood, ex-mayor, by upwards of 5000 of the working classes of Bolton. 30: Resignation of R. B. Armstrong, Esq., Q.C., the recorder of Bolton from the time of its incorporation. April 1: J. H. Ainsworth, Esq., Moss Bank, Halliwell, died, aged 64 years. May 6: Death of the Rev. C. Wright, M.A., of Silchester Rectory, near Basingstoke, formerly of Hill Top, Sharples, aged 66 years. 9: Bolton Improvement Bill received Royal assent. 17: Laying of the corner-stone of the new Poor-law Offices, Mawdsley-street. 20: Improvement of trade in Bolton; discontinuance of the operations of the Special Relief Committee. June 3: J. A. Russell, Esq., solicitor-general of the county palatine of Durham, appointed Recorder of Bolton. 9: Adam Hampson, Esq., surgeon, killed and several other residents of this town injured, in a railway accident at Staplehurst, Kent. July 12: Parliamentary election; votes recorded for Lieutenant-Col. Gray (C), 1033; Thomas Barnes (L), 979; Samuel Pope (L), 864; and William Gibb (C), 737,—the two former being elected. 16: Death of Thomas Andrews, Esq., aged 50 years, of the firm of Holden, Andrews, and Holden, solicitors. 29: Great scarcity of water. August 27: Death of Edmund Haworth, Esq., solicitor, aged 51, formerly chairman of the Board of Guardians. 31: Adoption of Local Government Act at Kersley. Oct. 18: Consecration of St. Matthew's Church, Little Lever. 30: Completion of the purchase of the Town Hall site; net cost £31,000. November 9: Richard Stockdale, Esq., re-elected Mayor. 25: Death of James Scowcroft, Esq., aged 77 years; Mayor of the borough in 1846-7. 27: Death of Mr. Richard Nightingale, in his 64th year, for several years an active member of the Bolton Town Council. Cattle plague in the Bolton division. Dec. 16: Consecration of St. Paul's Church, Deansgate. 22: Opening of the new Fish Market. Little Lever Church re-built.

1866. January 6 and 7: Great storm; doubling mill blown

down at Daubhill. 23 : Death of the Rev. James Spencer, aged 92, for nearly 50 years incumbent of St. Ann's Church, Turton. Death of Robt. Knowles, Esq., in his 77th year, one of the old Bolton worthies.—February 11th : Mr. Wm. Naisby, aged 81, a member of the first Town Council, died at Bowdon, Cheshire. 18 : Presentation of portrait to Mr Charles Hopwood, chairman of the Board of Guardians.—March 23 : Day of Humiliation on account of the cattle plague.—April 8 : Closing services at the Old Parish Church. 29 : Death of John Brown Holden, Esq., aged 60 years, for six years a member of the Town Council. — May 4 : Death of Gilbert James French, Esq., F.S.A., aged 62. Mr. French, as biographer of Samuel Crompton, was mainly instrumental in the erection of the Crompton Statue. Death of Mr. Thomas Entwisle, aged 62 ; one of the fathers of the Bolton Temperance Society. 24 : Opening of the Bolton Park, and "Heywood" Recreation Ground, by the Earl of Bradford.—July 16 : Turning of the first sod of the Wayoh Reservoir by the Mayor (Ald. Stockdale). 25 : Explosion of naphtha at the premises of Mr. Alfred Langshaw, chemist and druggist, Deansgate ; Mr. Langshaw and four other persons killed. September 1 : Execution of Thomas Grime, for the murder, on Jan. 3, 1863, of James Barton, engineer at the Ralk-house Colliery, Haigh.—October 3 : Henry Grimshaw, jockey, a native of Bolton, killed by being thrown out of his trap near Cambridge.—November 3 : Fire on the farm of Mr. Jas. Gillibrand, Tong-with-Haulgh ; eight cows burned to death. 7 : Inauguration of the new stores of the Bolton Co-operative Society, Limited, Bridge-street. 9 : Election of Fergus Ferguson, Esq., as Mayor. 10 : Explosion at Messrs. Thomas Wright and Son's collieries, Hanging Bank, Little Hulton ; seven lives lost and eighteen persons seriously injured. Dearness of provisions this year. Advance of wages of working classes generally. Rain fell on 195 days.

1867. January 7 : Death of A. R. Varley, Esq., solicitor, in the 40th year of his age, for six years a member of the Town Council. 18 : Death of Mr. John Gordon, accountant, aged 61 years, for nearly 30 years C.S. of the A.N.O.U. Oddfellows, Bolton Unity. 21 : William Ryder, Esq., spindle and fly maker, for six years a member of the Town Council, died at his residence, Ward Hill, Rivington, in the 59th year of his age.—Feb. 16 : Death of Mr. Henry Bradbury, printer and stationer, Deansgate, in the 51st year of his age. 19 : Wm. Cannon, Esq , an old Bolton worthy and for 12 years an alderman of the borough, died at his residence, Park Hill, in his 86th year. 21 : Death of George Piggot, Esq , in his 77th year, agent to the Earl of Bradford, and for six years an alderman of the borough.—March 7 : Dr. Chadwick offered £1000 towards the erection of a new Infirmary in the suburbs of the town, and another £1000 towards the purchase of the present Infirmary and buildings, and their conversion into a Public Museum and Library.—April 19 : Opening of the Congregational Church, Edgworth. 27 : Corner-stone of the new Parish Church laid by Peter Ormrod, Esq., of Halliwell Hall, the new church being erected at his sole expense. 28 : Fire at Sunnyside Mill, Daubhill, belonging to Messrs. Tootal Broadhurst, Lee, and Co. ; damage £10,000.—May 25 : Foundation-stone of St. James's Church, Waterloo-street, laid by the Rev. Canon Powell. Rev. Franklin Baker, M.A., formerly minister of

Bank-street Unitarian Chapel, died at Birmingham in his 67th
year. 29: Rev. Samuel Pagan, B.A., incumbent of Lever
Bridge, died in his 51st year.—June 5: Death of Mr.
James Haslam, at Birkdale, in the 61st year of his age, for six
years a member of the Bolton Town Council. 27: Death of
Mr. Boriase Wingfield, of East View, Sharples, in his 38th
year.—August 15: Trial of burglar-proof safes of Mr. S.
Chatwood, of Bolton, and Mr. S. C. Herring, of New York, at
the Paris Exhibition; the English engineers reported that
"Mr. Chatwood's was the best safe in its capability of resist-
ing burglars' appliances of any kind."—August 16: Death of
John Haslam, Esq., J.P., of Gilnow House, in his 51st year.—
September 20: Mr. John Rigby, biscuit manufacturer,
Bolton, killed by a falling tree whilst on a tour
near Killarney. 22: Opening of Independent Methodist
Chapel, Lee-lane, Horwich. — October 5: Inauguration
of Sunnyside Institute, Daubhill, erected by Messrs.
Tootal Broadhurst, Lee, and Co., at a cost of £3000.
11: Cotton mill of Messrs. John Haslam and Co., Chorley
Old-road, burnt down; damage, £20,000. 16: Resignation of
Mr. Jas. Harris, chief constable; Mr. Thos. Beech appointed as
his successor. 26: General reduction in the wages of spinners,
moulders, mechanics, millwrights, &c., in the borough.—Mr.
John Fawcett, professor of music, died, aged 77 years.—
Nov. 4: Councillor Edward Pilkington Holden, Springfield Paper
Works, aged 29, killed whilst superintending some of his machinery. 9: Election of Jas. Barlow, Esq., as Mayor. 23:
Execution of Allen, Larkin, and Gould, for the
murder of Police-sergeant Brett; 1032 special constables sworn
in at Bolton; the mills of the borough watched day and night
and the barracks in Fletcher-street guarded by 100 armed
volunteers. 25: Death of Mr. John Aspinwall, professor of music,
aged 61. 26: Fire at the mill of Messrs. Topp and Hindley,
Farnworth; damage £5000.—Death of Mr. John Gerrard, of Noble-
street, in his 67th year, believed to have been the oldest teetotal
blacksmith in the county. 29: Rev. David Hewitt, M.A.,
for 26 years incumbent of Horwich, died at Wrexham.
30: Rev. Joseph Dyson, pastor of the Congregational
Church, Farnworth, from 1818 to 1855, expired in his 87th year.
—December 1: Mr. James Morris, a chemist and druggist in
Deansgate for nearly half a century, died in the 67th year of his
age. 17: Fall of St. Paul's Church, Astley Bridge, whilst under-
going enlargement; William Carruthers, aged 57, foreman
joiner, killed, and two others injured.

1868.—Jan 1: Continuation of the Fenian agitation; 2161
special constables sworn in. 2: Munificent gift of £17,000 by Dr.
and Mrs. Chadwick for the erection of model dwellings for arti-
sans and the foundation of an Orphan Asylum. 29: Meeting at
Temperance Hall resolved to erect a statue by public subscription to Dr and Mrs. Chadwick.—February 15: Resignation of
Rev. Canon Thicknesse, M.A. vicar of Deane. 17: Remarkable
robbery of documents and coins from the corner stone
of the New Parish Church. 22: Opening of Commission Street Unitarian Chapel and Daubhill Wesleyan
School.—March 9: Parliamentary boundaries of Bolton extended. 18: Gift of £500 to the Infirmary and Dispensary by
James Stansfield, a warper at Gate Pike. 23: Death of James
Knowles, Esq., of Ainsworth House, aged 69, for 16 years
town clerk. 27: Gift of a plot of land in Haulgh by the Earl

of Bradford as a site for the Chadwick Orphanage.—April 2: Destruction by fire of Gilnow Mills, belonging to Messrs. P. R. Arrowsmith and Co.; damage, £50,000. 4: St. John's Church endowed £50 a year by Stephen Blair, Esq. 22: Opening of Wesleyan Chapel and Schools at Astley Bridge.—May 10: Closing services in Mawdsley-street Independent Chapel. June 19: Cotton mill of Messrs. Greenhalgh and Garstang, at Bradshaw, burnt down; damage, £2000. 20: Cotton mill of Messrs. R. and J. Howarth, at Edgworth, destroyed by fire; damage, £1500. —July 2: Fire at Mr. Michael Jackson's, Turton-street; damage £7000. 8: Foundation-stone laid of Claremont Baptist Chapel, St. George's-road. 14: Arrest of Mr. Wm. Murphy, the anti-Popery lecturer; disturbances apprehended, and special constables sworn in. 17: Mr. Murphy bound over by the magistrates to be of good behaviour for 12 months. 18: Corner-stone laid of St. Mark's Church, Fletcher-street. 27: Death of Stephen Temple, Esq., Q.C., attorney-general for the county palatine of Lancaster, aged 61 years. On the day of his death Mr. Temple was to have delivered his first address to the electors of this borough, for the representation of which he had been selected as a candidate after Dr. Chadwick had declined to stand. 30: Corner-stone laid of Independent Chapel, Mawdsley-street.—August 12: Opening of the new Post Office in Bradshawgate. Death of E. Langshaw, Esq., aged 59, one of the clerks to the magistrates of the Bolton division. 27: Major Bailey appointed joint clerk with Chris. Briggs, Esq., to the county justices. 28: Opening of the new Gas Offices, Hotel-street. 30: Opening of Victoria Wesleyan Methodist Sunday Schools.—September 3: Opening of Wesleyan Chapel, Tong-fold.—October 10: Opening of the Primitive Methodist Schools, Egyptian-street. 14: William Brierley, bookkeeper, of Kestor-street, and Nathaniel Morris, son of Mr. William Morris, Saddle Inn, Bradshawgate, fell over Crown-street Bridge into the River Croal, Brierley dying a few hours afterwards, and Morris having both thighs broken. 24: Death of Mr. John Cunliffe, proprietor of the *Bolton Guardian*, aged 60 years. 27: Death of Ald. Robert Heywood, of the Pike, aged 82. Deceased was for nearly 25 years one of the trustees for Great Bolton, Mayor of the borough 1839-40, and, on the Queen's marriage, was offered knighthood but declined it. For 55 years he was honorary secretary of the Infirmary and Dispensary. November 2: Riot in West Ward at the municipal election. 9: Ald. James Barlow re-elected Mayor. 10: Death of Edward Barlow, Esq., of the firm of Messrs. Dobson and Barlow, machinists. Mr Barlow was in the Town Council for 12 years; was appointed a borough magistrate in 1863; and was president of the Mechanics' Institution from 1862 to 1866. 17: Parliamentary election; number on register, 12,667. Votes recorded for John Hick, Esq. (C) 6062, Lieut.-Col. Gray (C) 5842, Thomas Barnes, Esq. (L) 5451, and Samuel Pope, Esq. (L) 5436,—the two former being elected. Before the close of the poll, there was a riot in Newtown, and the military were sent for from Bury. 25: Gift to the town of a public playground off Water-loo-street, by S. D. Darbishire and C. J. Darbishire, Esqrs.—December 7: Inaugural exhibition at the New Mechanics' Institution, in Mawdsley-street. 27: Terrific gale; the new Baptist Chapel, St. George's-road, the new branch schools of

St. George's, in Mount-street, and a weaving shed at Gate Pike belonging to Messrs. R. Crompton and Co., partially blown down, damage over £1000.—Trade generally flat throughout the borough.

1869. January 27: Death of Mr. James Harris, aged 61, for 24 years superintendent of police for this borough. 30: Dr. Chadwick transferred £5000 in consols for the extension of his charity, making with the £17,000 previously presented by him a total of £22,000.—February 1: Destructive gale in Bolton, and considerable damage to property. 12: Conservative banquet to celebrate the return of Messrs. Hick and Gray. 23: Presentation of silver epergnes to Messrs. Barnes and Pope, the Liberal candidates at the preceding general election.—March 3: Samuel Pope, Esq., appointed borough recorder, in place of J. A. Russell, Esq., Q.C., resigned. 11: St. James's Church opened by licence of the Bishop of Manchester. 12: Sarah Crawford sentenced to death at Manchester Assizes for drowning her child in Messrs. Ainsworth's lodge, at Great Lever; sentence subsequently commuted to penal servitude for life. 15: A shock of earthquake felt in Bolton and other places throughout the north of England—April 4: Death of Mr. Johnson Lomax, for many years chairman of the Gas Company, aged 83. 17: Close of the Exhibition at the Mechanics' Institution; profit on account of building fund, £641 14s. 9d. 18: Closing services at All Saints' Church, prior to re-erection. 21: Opening of new Wesleyan Chapel, at Westhoughton. 21: Working Men's Club, Bank House, closed. 28: Fire at the manufactory of Messrs. Thomas Pearson and Son, Dean-street; damage over £1000 —May 4: Presentation to the Rev. Joseph Lowe, M.A., on his retirement from the vicarage of Holy Trinity. 8: Corner-stone laid of Bolton Moor Temperance Hall. 9: Rev. Henry Haworth succeeded Rev. J. Lowe as vicar of Holy Trinity. 13: Fire at the cotton mill of Messrs. Little and Smith, at Belmont; damage £20,000. 28: Fire at the shop of Mr. Tookey, provision dealer, Market Hall; damage £1000. June 4: Thomas Pollitt, a wheelwright, and John Proctor, a salesman, drowned by the upsetting of a boat on the canal.—July 1: The new Mechanics' Institution opened to the public. 2: Opening of the new County Court, Mawdsley-street. 10: Inspector Holland appointed superintendent of the Bolton petty sessional division, in place of Mr. J. R. Scott, resigned. 13: Government inquiry into the endowed charities in the parish of Bolton. 19: Visit of the Prince and Princess of Wales to Worsley Hall. 26: Inauguration at Worsley of a memorial to the late Countess of Ellesmere.—August 6: Mr. James Taylor, an alderman of the borough, died at his residence, Chorley Old-road, aged 62. 7: Fire at the bleachworks of Messrs. R. Ainsworth, Son, and Co., Halliwell; damage £2000. 18: Opening of the Wesleyan Chapel, Halliwell-road.—September 1: Commencement of first beer licensing sessions for the borough of Bolton; 73 licences refused. 8: First sessions for granting beerhouse licences in the county; 41 certificates refused. 11: Opening of the Bolton Moor Temperance Hall. 25: Henry Whittle, a handloom weaver, of Westhoughton, murdered his daughter-in-law, Ellen Whittle, with an axe, and then committed suicide by cutting his own throat. 30: Death of James Hardcastle, Esq., J.P., of Firwood, aged 68.— October 16: Opening of the Little Lever Co-operative Stores.

30: Corner stone laid of All Saints' New Church.—November 6: Corner stone laid of St. Luke's Church, Halliwell. 9: Councillor Thomas Walmsley elected Mayor, being the first Conservative Mayor since 1852.—December 2: Opening of Claremont Baptist Chapel, St. George's-road. 29: Opening of St. Thomas's Church School, Moses Gate.—Trade generally dull throughout the year.

1870.—January 16: Death of Harrison Blair, Esq., J.P., of Peel Hall, Little Hulton, aged 58. 18: Peter Ainsworth, Esq., of Smithills Hall, died, aged 79; represented Bolton in Parliament from 1835 to 1847. Death of John Heaton, Esq., of Marsh-fold, aged 50.—February 5: Telegraphs came under supervision of Government. Opening of Mount-street Sunday School. 13: Died at Springfield House, Chorley-new Road, John Orton, Esq., aged 66, Mayor of the borough 1859-60. 14: Opening of the Horwich branch railway. 21: Death of Mr. John Lomax, auctioneer.—March 9: Opening of Mawdsley-street Independent Chapel. 16: Election of James Broughton Edge, Esq., barrister-at-law, as coroner for the Bolton division of the county.—April 1: Died, aged 79 years, the Rev. William Probert, for 49 years minister of Walmsley Unitarian Chapel. 2: Interment of Mr. John Barlow, a wealthy landed proprietor, of Lower Crow Trees, Entwisle, in the centre of a field on the Entwisle Hall estate. Presentation of the portrait of Mr. Ald. Jas. Barlow (ex-mayor), by his workpeople, to the Mayor and Corporation. Death of Mr. George Smith, of Darcy Lever, the father of Wesleyan Methodism in that locality. 9: Death of Mr. Peter Greenwell, aged 67, a well-known character in Bolton. Death of Mr. Ald. Peter Skelton, aged 61. 23: William Yates, stonemason, killed by a fall from the chimney of the Bullfield cotton mill.—May 2: Westhoughton Co-operative Cotton Company's mill destroyed by fire; damage from £25,000 to £30,000. 23: Death of Mr. George Slater, of The Holmes, Sharples, aged 87 years—the last surviving member of the Bolton Light Horse Volunteers.—June 16: Destructive thunderstorm in Bolton and neighbourhood. 21: Destruction by fire of the old Mossfield Mill, Farnworth, belonging to Messrs. Joseph Whittam and Sons; damage £20,000.—July 4: Death of Stephen Blair, Esq., of Mill Hill House, Bolton, aged 65 years, representative of Bolton in Parliament from 1848 to 1852, and first Conservative mayor of Bolton (1845-6). On his death Mr. Blair left £30,000 for the erection and endowment of a "Blair Hospital." 16: Death of Rev. E. Quant, secretary of the British Temperance League, aged 58 years. 23: Died at Penwortham Priory, near Preston, Mr. James Greenroyd, aged 66 years, an alderman of the borough from 1844 to 1856.—August 5: Died at Newport House, aged 33, Mr. Councillor G. E. Gorton, sharebroker. 8: Establishment of The Bolton Daily Chronicle. 17: Death of Mr. Joseph Crompton, aged 64, a well-known temperance advocate. 24: Consecration of St. Bartholomew's Church, Westhoughton, erected by Mr. John Seddon, at a cost of about £6000.—September 6: Severe thunderstorm in Bolton and neighbourhood; John Morris, travelling pedlar, being frightened to death by it in Little Lever. 26: Mr. Henry Lomax, of Ainsworth Vale Bleachworks, accidentally dragged at the heels of his horse for a quarter of a mile and killed. 27: Explosion at the Wheat Sheaf Colliery, Pendlebury, belonging to Messrs. A. Knowles and Son; six persons fatally burned.—October 5: Died in Water-street,

aged 72, Mr. John Lomax, one of the first town councillors.　10 :
Death of James Arrowsmith, Esq., of Sea Bank House, Southport,
aged 72, a member of the first Town Council and mayor of this
borough 1840-41.　13 : Died, aged 69, Mr. Richard Dunderdale,
one of the first councillors elected for Bolton.　21 : Death of
the Rev. George Airey, incumbent of Peel, aged 34.　27 : Opening
of the Conservative Club, Bradford Buildings; cost about
£10,000.—November 9 : Thomas Walmsley, Esq., re-elected Mayor
of Bolton.　26 : Mr. George Bell, of the firm of Messrs. Hick,
Hargreaves, and Co., of Bolton, and his wife, killed, with five
other persons, in a railway collision at Harrow.　30 : Unopposed
election of School Board for Bolton.—December 8 : Opening of
new Wesleyan Chapel at Kersley Mount.　14 : Destruction by fire
of Mount Pleasant Mill, in Bury-street, occupied by Mr. John
Hoyle; damage £15,000 to £20,000.　Trade generally better than
in 1869.

1871.—January 5 : Lark Mill, Farnworth, partially destroyed
by fire, damage £2000.—February 1 : Victoria Mills, Elton, belonging to Messrs. J. P. Ede and Co., destroyed by fire; five men
burned to death; damage, £50,000.　14 : Mad dog bit several
persons in Bolton, Ann Bradbury, aged 4 years, of Chapel-street,
dying on 4th March, and Jos. W. Houghton, aged 5, of Waterloo-
street, dying on the 12th of that month.—Feb. & March : Presen-
tations by gentry and congregation to Rev. T. Berry, 30 years
Vicar of Christ church, and 14 years President of Poor Protection
Society, on preferment to the Vicarage of St. Werburg's, Derby.
Mar. 4 : Fall of the roof of Mr. Chas. Adams's circus; 2 men killed,
and 5 others injured.　17 : Shock of earthquake in Bolton and
neighbourhood.　22 : Opening of All Saints' new church.—April
3 : Decennial census.　Population of the Municipal borough of
Bolton, 82,857 ; Parliamentary borough, 92,655 ; Bolton Union,
169,402. 12 : Death of Mr. Richard Wallwork, West Bank, aged 60,
who was in the Council from 1855 to 1861.　25 : St. Mark's Church
consecrated.—May 8 : Opening of the new Trinity-street Station
of the Lancashire and Yorkshire Railway Company.　18 : St.
James's Church consecrated.　27 : Gunpowder explosion on
Aspull Moor; six persons dreadfully burned, two of whom died
next morning.　29 : A.M.D. in Bolton of the Order of Druids.—
June 1-5 : Encampment of the 27th Lancashire Rifle Volunteers at Lytham.　5 : Died, aged 68, George Mallett, Esq.,
F.R.C.S., of Silverwell House.　20 : Fearful storm ; woman
killed by lightning at Aspull, and three cows killed at Westhoughton.　29 : Consecration of Bolton new Parish Church,
erected by Peter Ormrod, Esq., of Halliwell Hall, at an expense
of between £30,000 and £40,000.—July 1 : Consecration of St.
Stephen's Church, Kersley.　Cotton mills of Bolton commenced
closing at one o'clock on Saturdays.　8 : Opening of Fern-street
Wesleyan School Chapel.　14 : Death of Mr. James Best, brush
manufacturer, Manchester Road, aged 65, for several years a
representative of Exchange Ward in the Town Council, and
Chairman of the Board of Guardians.　22 : Mr. Ald. James
Barlow offered to Wesleyan Conference the use for seven years
of a farm of 76 acres at Edgworth, for the training of children
to agricultural pursuits.—August 7 : The Bolton School Board
reported that the number of children requiring instruction in
this borough was 17,059, whilst the available accommodation
was 14,896 ; they therefore recommended that board schools be
established in West, Bradford, Derby, and East Wards.　13 :
Died at Great Lever, aged 88, Mr. James Longworth, guardian

for Farnworth. 15: Bolton tradesmen decided to close their places of business one day in August in each year. 25: Three boys killed by a fly-wheel falling upon them at Smith's Old Colliery, Great Lever. 26: Opening of the new schools of St. Ann's Church, Turton. Alarming prevalence of foot and mouth disease in Bolton and neighbourhood.—September 4: Closing of the Great Moor-street station of the London and North-Western Railway Company. 12: Death of Mr. John Makin, of Blackburn-street, aged 77; a much respected inhabitant of Bolton, and for a great number of years cashier at Messrs. Ormrod and Hardcastle's; it is stated that it was a pamphlet published by Mr. Makin which led to the appointment of a Select Committee of the House of Commons in 1834 to inquire into the distress of the handloom weavers in the manufacturing districts. 13: The Borough of Bolton divided into two portions for sanitary purposes. 20: Death of Mr. Joseph Marsden, of West Bank, aged 52, one of the largest builders in Lancashire. 22: Died, aged 87, Mr. John Lomax, of Rose Cottage, Deane, considered to be the last survivor of Colonel Fletcher's volunteers.—October 4: Interred in the Cemetery, Mrs. Elizabeth Allen, aged 76, of Kay-street, widow of Mr. Thos. Allen, tailor, the first person buried in the Cemetery after its opening, on the 20th December, 1856; during that period nearly 25,000 persons had been interred in the ground. 9: Died, aged 66, Mr. Ralph Fryer, cabinet maker and upholsterer, Folds-road, a musical composer, and an intimate friend of Samuel Crompton, the inventor of the spinning mule. 11: In consequence of the prevalence of small-pox, the Town Council resolved to erect a temporary hospital in Spa-fields. 20: Died, aged 59, Mr. William Lomax, auctioneer and valuer, Stella View, and high bailiff to the Bolton County Court. 26: Thomas Davies, aged 52, counterpane weaver, of Breightmet, strangled his wife in bed, and then committed suicide by cutting his own throat. The Bolton School Board, by 7 to 6, adopted bye-laws providing for payment of fees to denominational schools. Complimentary banquet to W. F. Hulton, Esq. at the Conservative Club. 27: Opening of the new Wholesale Market, in Great Moor-street.—November 9: W. W. Cannon, Esq., elected Mayor; for the first time since 1850 the Conservatives were able also to elect six of their own party as aldermen. 17: Died at Torquay, aged 77, Sir Joshua Walmsley, M.P. for Bolton from 1849 to 1852. 24: Death of Mr. Samuel Rawsthorn, of Bradford Road, Haulgh, aged 37, formerly one of the Conservative representatives of Exchange Ward. 25: Inauguration of the Bolton Republican Club; an attempt to prevent Mr. George Odger, of London, from speaking was defeated; and a large crowd afterwards assembled outside, and pelted some of the more active Republican members with rotten eggs and flour bags, Mr. Odger making his escape by a back door. 30: Alarming riot at the Temperance Hall, on the occasion of an address by Sir Charles Dilke, M.P., on "Representation and Registration;" considerable damage to the Hall, several persons seriously injured, one man, named Wm. Schofield, of Smith-street, dying on the 7th December from the effects of his injuries; at the inquest a verdict of "Manslaughter against some person unknown" was returned.—December 13: The Town Council unanimously resolved to purchase the works and undertaking of the Bolton Gas Company, and to apply for powers to incorporate Daubhill within the borough. Trade generally good throughout the year. Foot and mouth disease and small-pox abating.

1872.

January 1: Petition of 6000 persons to the Home Secretary praying for an inquiry into the Dilke riot. Adoption of the nine hours system by the iron trades of Bolton. 3: Thomas McCarte, better known as "Massarti, the lion tamer," worried by lions at Manders's Menagerie, on the Market Square. 7: Mr. James Barry, one of the first representatives of Church Ward in the Town Council, died at Green Bank, Heaton, aged 75. 13: Died at Moses Gate, aged 68, Mr. Wm. Hayhurst, auctioneer, one of the originators of the Bolton Market Hall. 21: Adam L. Haworth, Esq., father of the legal profession in Bolton, died at Lytham, aged 82. 31: Explosion of fire-damp at Trencherbone Colliery, Ladyshore, Little Lever, by which a young man named Samuel Morris, of Hag End, Haulgh, was killed, and four other persons were injured.—February 1: Seventeen persons summoned before the Borough Magistrates, on three charges—viz.: riot, damaging the Temperance Hall, and manslaughter of William Schofield; the examination extended into the 10th day, when six of the defendants (including Major Hesketh) were discharged, and eight committed to the assizes for riot,—the charges against the remaining three defendants having been previously withdrawn. 5: Transfer of the British School, All Saints'-street, to the Bolton School Board. 15: Rev. J. C. Nesbitt, of the Lancashire Independent College, ordained minister of Duke's-alley Independent Chapel, Bolton. 26: Destruction of Gilnow Old Mill (Messrs. Salmon and Taylor's) by fire; damage about £30,000. 29: Serious floods in the Wayoh Valley; bursting of an embankment at the new Waterworks there. —March 14: Inaugural Meeting of the Bolton Church Defence Association. 18-19: Trial of the Dilke rioters at Manchester assizes; the jury, being unable to agree, were discharged, and the defendants were bound over to appear at the next assizes, when they were discharged, no evidence being offered against them. 24: Opening of St. Stephen's United Presbyterian Church, Bradford-street, Haulgh. 28: Terrible explosion of fire-damp at Lovers' Lane Colliery, Atherton; 27 persons killed and 13 injured. 29: Opening of the Victoria Wesleyan Chapel, Grecian-street.—April 1: Co-operative Congress in Bolton. 27: Adoption of Local Government Act at Little Lever. Mr. J. Arrowsmith Walsh, professor of music, St. George's Road, died, aged 48. 29: Adoption of the Local Government Act at Little Hulton.— May 2-4: Mr. C. S. Whitmore, Q.C., and Mr. J. B. Maule, Q.C., by direction of the Home Secretary, instituted an inquiry into the Dilke riot; the commissioners entirely exonerated Major Hesketh from the particular charges made against him. 9: Adoption of the Local Government Act at Blackrod. 18: Dreadful explosion of gunpowder at the house and shop of George Hunt, provision dealer and clogger, corner of Chequerbent-lane, Westhoughton; Mrs. Hunt was killed, and her husband, son, daughter, and an apprentice severely injured. 20: A.M.C. of the National Independent Order of Oddfellows held in Bolton. 22: Adoption of the Local Government Act at Aspull. 23: Adoption of the Local Government Act at Turton.—June 1: Publication of the Home Secretary's report on the commission of inquiry into the Dilke riot; though "there was a most unreasonable delay in action on the part of the magistrates," Mr. Bruce was of opinion that they "acted according to the best of their honest judgment," and that "no charge against any individual magistrate had any substantial foundation." Adoption of the Local Government Act at Horwich. 19: The Market Square re-named "Town Hall Square." 29: Adoption of the Local Government Act at Westhoughton. 30: Bolton Gasworks transferred to Corporation. — July 3: Opening of the new Wesleyan School in Draycott-street. 12: Destructive thunderstorm in Bolton and the neighbourhood; great floods at Turton, works partially destroyed, and about £10,000 damage sustained. 18: Royal assent to the Bolton Corporation Bill, providing for the transfer of the Gasworks to the Corporation on June 30, 1872; the incorporation of Deanhill (Rumworth) within the borough, which took place on the same day the Royal assent was given; and the alteration of the ward boundaries in 1873. 26: Mr. Finlay Fraser, a well-known botanist and entomologist, died in Edmund-street, aged 88.— August 3: Terrible collision near Clifton Junction, on the Bolton and Manchester Railway, between an "express" and a coal train; four persons killed and 16 injured. 17: The new Licensing Act put into operation in Bolton. 28: Last meeting of the Bolton Gas Company. Resignation of C. Briggs, Esq., one of the clerks to the county justices of the Bolton division, and appointment of A. Bailey Esq., as sole clerk; the magistrates unanimously recommended that Mr. Briggs should be placed upon the commission of the peace, which recommendation was afterwards confirmed by the Lord-Lieutenant.—September 4: Another terrible thunderstorm in Bolton and district; a pleasure party struck by lightning on Turton Moor,—one man being killed, and two other persons seriously injured. 5: Mr. Thomas Hardman, professor of music, died at his residence, Nelson Square, aged 50. 7: Peel Mill No. 1, Turton-street, Little Bolton, destroyed by fire; damage about £30,000, and several of the workpeople injured. 11-13: Manchester and Liverpool Agricultural Society's Show at Bolton. 12: Visit of the Tichborne Claimant to Bolton. 25: Weekly half-holiday of tradesmen of the town commenced. Serious fire at Messrs. T. Barnes and Co.'s cotton mill, Gladstone Road, Farnworth; damage £5000. — October 13: Opening of the new Welsh Presbyterian Chapel, Clarence-street, Little Bolton. 17: Edward Barlow and Henry Crompton killed by the falling of some flags at Eagley. 20: Opening of Blackbank-street Congregational School-Church. 26: Gift of £3000 by John Green, Esq., towards the erection of a new church in connection with the Mount-street district of St. George's. Waterloo Mills, Little Bolton, belonging to Messrs. T. Cross and Co., burned down; damage £30,000.— November 1: First election in Bolton under the Ballot Act; ten Conservatives and two Liberal councillors were returned in the six contested wards; two Conservatives and one Liberal being returned without a contest for the new ward of Rumworth. 9: W. W. Cannon, Esq., re-elected Mayor. Consecration of the new church at Bradshaw by the Bishop of Manchester. 13: Arrival of Sergeant Bates, with the American flag, in Bolton. 15: Died at Kersley, aged 66, the Rev. W. Woodman, for 33 years pastor of the New Jerusalem Church, Kersley, and controversialist, lecturer, and author. 17: Died, aged 74, T. G. Horridge, Esq., of The Raikes, Great Lever, one of the oldest bleachers in the county. Opening of the new Independent Methodist Chapel, Noble-street. 18; Appointment of the Rev. Burman Cassin, M.A., vicar of St. George's, Battersea, to the incumbency of St. Paul's, Bolton. Died at his residence, Claremont, Exeter, aged 80, Sir John Bowring, LL.D., F.R.S., who represented Bolton in Parliament from 1841 to 1849. John Osborne, Esq., Q.C., judge of the Bolton County Court, died at his residence at Prestwich, aged 62.—8; Mr. Alex. Jones, cashier at The Chronicle Office, died, aged 37; he was for many years treasurer and secretary of the Bolton Cricket Club, and also secretary of the Bolton Philharmonic Society. 9; At the Manchester assizes, John Entwistle was sentenced to 18 months' imprisonment for stealing cloth at Bolton; and William Crook was also sentenced to a like period of imprisonment for stealing cloth and unlawfully wounding Detective Dearden, by shooting him. 13; Complimentary banquet by the junior magistrates of the Bolton petty sessional division of the county to W. F. Hulton, Esq., senior acting magistrate on the Bolton bench. 17; First contested election for Rumworth Ward; Conservative candidate (Mr. J. R. Simpson) returned. 21; Death of Mr. S. N. Bancroft, surgeon, Mawdsley-street, aged 70. 26; Re-opening of the Temperance Hall, after enlargement. Crompton Hutton, Esq., of the Inner Temple, appointed County Court judge for Bolton.

1873.

JANUARY.—1; New Church schools opened at Daubhill by the Bishop of Manchester. 8; Terrible accident at the Bolton Iron and Steel Works, by which one man was killed and six injured, through the breaking of a fly wheel.

FEBRUARY.—5; Dr. Livy appointed Medical Officer of Health for Bolton at a salary of £300 a year. 7; Terrible collision near Chequerbent, on the London and North-Western Railway; two brakesmen killed. 22; Opening of the new schools of St. Saviour's Church, Ringley. 25; Welcome to the Rev. Burman Cassin, M.A., incumbent of St. Paul's.

MARCH.—10; Eight cows burned to death on the farm of Mr. Jas. Gillibrand, at Tong-with-Haulgh.

APRIL.—5; Memorial stone of the Halliwell Road Wesleyan Schools laid by Mr. G. Knowles. 7; Mr. J. Barlow gave £5000 to the Edgworth Home. 8; Miss Knowles, eldest daughter of Mr. J. Knowles, of Heaton Grange, thrown off her horse near Lytham, receiving injuries from which she died on the 15th. 11; Union Sunday School, Entwisle, opened. 14; Subscription Department of the Public Free Library transferred to the Exchange News Room, Town Hall Square.

MAY.—1; Boring of the Entwisle tunnel, which is 3050 yards long, completed. 17; Foundation stone of the Little Lever Congregational Sunday School laid by Mr. Thomas Barnes.

JUNE.—5; Opening of the Town Hall by the Prince of Wales. His Royal Highness was accompanied by the Princess of Wales, and there was a grand procession, followed by a banquet at which the Prince and Princess were present. In the evening the town was brilliantly illuminated. Towards the decoration and illumination of the town the Corporation voted £1500, but only £1120 of this was spent. Total cost of the building, £166,416. Medals struck to commemorate the occasion.

JULY.—8: Inauguration of the Bolton Certified Industrial School. 22: Terrible thunderstorm in Bolton; two lads killed off Cannon-street and great damage to property.

AUGUST.—1: The Chadwick Statue, Town Hall Square, erected by subscription of 17,000 inhabitants, unveiled by James Barlow, Esq., of Edgworth; cost £950; medal struck to commemorate the event. 13: Salary of Mr. R. Winder, magistrates' clerk, increased from £550 to £750 per annum.

SEPTEMBER.—25: Farnworth Parish Church re-opened after being beautified and enlarged at a cost of £4000. 28: Rev. W. H. Davison, pastor of the Congregational Church, St. George's Road, preached his farewell sermon.

OCTOBER.—1: Three men scalded to death in the Smithfold Colliery, Little Hulton, through an escape of steam. 8: Shocking death of a man named George Manley from hydrophobia.

NOVEMBER.—First election under the revised ward boundaries, North Ward being formed out of West Ward, and other alterations made. In seven wards there were contests, which resulted in ten Conservatives and five Liberals being elected, and for the third place in North Ward a scrutiny was demanded, Messrs. J. Cooper, L, G. Ryder, C, and F. Hamilton, L, having received an equal number of votes. Eventually Ald. Walmsley, the presiding alderman for the ward, gave his casting vote in favour of Mr. Cooper, Liberal. Mr. Poole, Conservative, was returned unopposed for Rumworth Ward. 10: J. Marsden, Esq., elected Mayor of Bolton. 19: Foundation stone of Pike's-lane Board School laid by T. L. Rushton, Esq., chairman of the Board. 25: Election of new School Board, resulting in the return of six Church, two Wesleyan, two Roman Catholic, and three Unsectarian candidates. The following were the numbers for each candidate:—Rev. Canon Powell (Churchman), 13,055; Rev. Canon Carter (Roman Catholic), 9079; Herbert Cross, M.A., Oxon. (Churchman), 8585; George Jas. Healy (Roman Catholic), 8532; John Leigh Taylor (Wesleyan), 8506; Robert Nivin Cottrill (Churchman), 8470; Thomas Moscrop (Wesleyan), 8395; Richard Knill Freeman (Churchman), 7952; John Morris (Churchman), 7754; Henry Lee (Unsectarian), 7611; Thomas William Heelis (Churchman), 7161; William Abbatt (Unsectarian), 6857; and Stephen Winkworth (Unsectarian), 6419; the unsuccessful candidates being Messrs. Robert Taylor, J. S. Holdsworth, and Francis Taylor. 29.

DECEMBER—13: Double railway collision on the Lancashire and Yorkshire line between the Gilnow crossing and Lady Bridge; about a dozen persons injured. Trade generally very good.

OBITUARY FOR 1873.

January 6: Death of Mr. Thomas Fildes Johnson, cotton spinner, Daubhill, Liberal representative in the Council for Bradford Ward from 1856 to 1859. 7: Mr. Thomas Scowcroft, provision dealer, Bradshawgate, Liberal representative in the Council for Church Ward from 1854 to 1860.—February 10: Mr. David Jones, of Blackburn Road, for 27 years sub-inspector of factories for this district.—April 15: Mr. John Vickers, counterpane manufacturer, and a member of the first Town Council, aged 77 years. 19: Mr. Alfred Bird, for upwards of 20 years landlord of the Lever's Arms Hotel, Nelson Square, aged

55 years.—June 4: aged 30, the Rev. W. Mackay Gordon, M.A., minister of St. Andrew's Presbyterian Church, Bolton.— July 9: Robert Walsh, Esq., J.P., aged 82. He was a representative of East Ward in the first Town Council, and when he left the Council in 1865 he was an alderman. He was also included in the first list of borough magistrates, and he was Mayor for the year 1842-3. In politics he was a Liberal. 17: Mr. Thomas Myerscough, aged 83. Deceased was a member of the Town Council for many years, and also held other public offices. He was a Conservative in politics.— Oct. 11: James Cullen, Esq., aged 44 years, died at his residence, Chorley New Road, after a very brief illness.—November 3: Mr. Jas. Parkinson, auctioneer and valuer, Newport-street, formerly a member of the Town Council, and a prominent local advocate of advanced Radicalism, died very suddenly, aged 63 years.— December 4: Died at sea, on his way to Alexandria, Robert Smalley, Esq., J.P., aged 57 years; for several years a member of the Town Council and a Borough Magistrate. Mr. Smalley was an advanced Liberal and an ardent temperance reformer. His body was buried at sea. 17: aged 49, Mr. James Ashton, of the Robin Hood Hotel, Ashburner-street, one of the originators of the Chadwick Statue.

1874.

JANUARY.—1: Man killed in Bradshawgate by an omnibus. 6: Home Rule meeting at the Temperance Hall. 8: A vertical boiler at Mr. Ald. Walmsley's Atlas Forge burst, by which six persons were killed and 18 injured. The damage was estimated at nearly £5000. A public subscription was opened for the relief of the sufferers, supplemented by collections in various places of worship. 10: Inquiry by Captain Tyler, of the Board of Trade, into the double railway collision at Gilnow on Saturday, Dec. 13th, 1873; some extraordinary revelations were made touching the manner in which trains were despatched one after another between Bolton and Lostock. 11: Rev. C. Cronshaw, incumbent-elect of St. Matthew's, held his first services in the Mount-street School. 17: Messrs. J. K. Cross, O. Heaton, S. Winkworth, and C. Taylor placed on the commission of the peace for the borough. 21: The new Unitarian Sunday and day schools in Bank-street inaugurated.

FEBRUARY.—4: Parliamentary election: John Hick (C) 5967, J. K. Cross (L) 5782, Col. Wm. Gray (C) 5650, and Jas. Knowles (L) 5440; Messrs. Hick and Cross elected. 7: Mr. E. Sergeant appointed Medical Officer of Health and Borough Analyst, at a salary of £400 a year. 10: Three horses burnt to death at Ashton Field Farm, Little Hulton. 26: Wm. Tuke, surveyor, Pendleton, killed whilst on the line at Gilnow.

MARCH.—4: Mr. E. M. Garstang appointed house surgeon at the Infirmary. 16: Committee appointed to procure subscriptions towards the Bengal Famine Fund. The sum collected was £2185 7s. 3d. 17: Thomas Holt sentenced to twelve months' imprisonment at Manchester assizes for the manslaughter of his wife at Breightmet on the 3rd December, 1873.

APRIL.—8: Bazaar in the Albert Hall in aid of the Cricket Club fund, realising upwards of £1200. 29: Explosion of metal at the Bolton Iron and Steel Works, by which one man was killed and four badly injured.

MAY.—6: Strike of 2000 colliers in the Bolton district in consequence of notice of a reduction in wages of 20 per cent. The men remained out for a time not exceeding in the longest cases a month, and then returned to work at a reduction of about 10 per cent. Opening of St. James's New Schools, to accommodate 1087 children. 13: Welcome to the Rev. C. C. Coe, of Leicester, the new pastor of Bank-street unitarian Chapel. 28: Mr. Justice Mellor commenced the trial, in the Bolton Town Hall, of the petition against the return of Mr. J. K. Cross, Liberal representative of the borough. The allegations were bribery, treating, undue influence, and other unlawful acts. The trial lasted nearly three days. The petition was dismissed, but Mr. Cross had to bear his own costs so far as related to the conduct of his personating agents and the sending out of the railway passes, the learned Judge being of opinion that those acts were of a character "which might fairly be considered by persons advising the petitioners as likely to void the election." With regard to two alleged cases of bribery, the petitioners were ordered to bear Mr. Cross's costs. Mr. Cross therefore retained his seat. The 27th Lancashire Rifle Volunteer corps encamped at Lytham for the fourth time, under the command of Lieut.-Col. Bailey.

JUNE.—18: The cotton waste warehouse of Messrs. Peter Ward and Son, Kay-street, destroyed by fire; damage over £1000.

JULY.—1: Welcome at the Blackbank-street Congregational School to the Rev. J. E. Clayton, the new minister. 3: Farewell tea party to the Rev. E. Franks, Methodist New Connexion. 4: Corner stone laid of Bertinshaw Wesleyan Chapel. 11: Closing tea party in Mawdsley-street Independent School, prior to its demolition for the Old-acres improvement.

AUGUST.—5: Corner stone of St. Paul's Church, Little Hulton, laid by Lord Kenyon. Opening of the new Congregational Chapel, Egerton. 10: Rev. S. Prenter, B.A., ordained to the pastorate of St. Andrew's Presbyterian Church, Bowker's-row. Cutting of the first sod on the site of St. Matthew's Church, by the Rev. C. Cronshaw.

SEPTEMBER.—12: Great strike in the Bolton cotton trade in consequence of notices of a reduction of 5 per cent in wages. The notices were posted in 88 mills, but in seven they were withdrawn in a few days. In 53 mills the notices were not given. The number of hands affected was about 11,575; and the cost to the Self-actor Minders and Operative Cotton Spinners' Associations was about £2200. On Wednesday, the 16th, it was agreed to refer the points in dispute to Mr. J. A. Russell, Q.C., judge of the Manchester County Court, and the men resumed work the following week at the old prices. Mr. Russell held his inquiry on the 9th, 10th, and 11th of October, in the Town Hall, and on the 20th October sent in his award in favour of the masters, so that the wages of the hands were forthwith reduced 5 per cent. 16: Rev. Charles Berry, of Airedale College, appointed pastor of St. George's Road Congregational Church.

OCTOBER.—3: Miss Howell, of Great Lever, presented £5000 towards the erection of a new church at Burnden, in addition to £1000 which she had previously given. 7: Bazaar in the Albert Hall in aid of the debt on Wesley Chapel, opened by Mr. Hick, M.P.; sum realised, £2363 16s. 8d. 21: Organ in the Albert Hall opened by Mr. W. T. Best, of Liverpool; its cost was about £4000. 26: Grand conversaziones by the Mayor and Mayoress (Mr. and Mrs. Marsden) in the Town Hall, to which upwards of 500 invitations were issued.

NOVEMBER.—1: Rev. Plunket Mooney, B.A., vicar of St. Peter's, Halliwell, preached his farewell sermons. Serious floods at Astley Bridge; man drowned. 9: Ald. J. Marsden re-elected Mayor. 14: Public tea party in St. James's School to welcome the Rev. Robert Lever, B.A., as curate of the parish. 18: Great Conservative demonstration at the Temperance Hall, and presentation of a service of plate worth £350 to Colonel Gray, in recognition of his services to the borough during the seventeen years he had represented it in the House of Commons.

DECEMBER.—5: Rev. J. H. Gibbon, B.A., of St. Mark's, Wrexham, appointed incumbent of St. Luke's, Halliwell. 7: The Chadwick Orphanage opened. 9: Flood at Kersley, by which over £3000 damage was done at the dye mills of Mr. Mark Fletcher, Stoneclough Brow. 14: Conference at the Swan Hotel between Mr. Robert Baker, inspector of factories, the certifying surgeons of the Bolton district, and a number of members of the Short-time Committee, with respect to the passing of children as full-timers. 16: Marriage at Clapham of John Hick, Esq., M.P., to Rebecca Maria, only daughter of Edmund Ashworth, Esq, J.P., of Egerton Hall. Presentation of a silver cradle to the Mayor (Ald. J. Marsden) and the Mayoress, to commemorate the birth of their daughter during the first year of his Worship's mayoralty. 19: Twenty-two acres of land in Darley Park transferred from Miss Rawson to the Farnworth Burial Board for a cemetery, at a cost of £7074 14s. 4d. 21: Consecration of St. Luke's Church, Halliwell, by the Bishop of Manchester. 24: William Baker, 'bus driver, accidentally killed by falling from his 'bus in Market-street, Farnworth. Very severe frost. Trade somewhat dull during the year, following the late high prices.

OBITUARY FOR 1874.

January 15: Mr. Richard P. Makin, accountant, aged 52 years. 16: Mr. Wm. Smith, Derby-street, the oldest master tailor in Bolton.—Feb. 11: Mr. Thomas Hodson, farmer, Tynesbank, Little Hulton. He served for many years in the offices of overseer, poor-law guardian, surveyor of taxes, and churchwarden.—March 1: Mr. Thomas Booth, of Churchgate, in his 65th year, one of the oldest musicians in Bolton. 7: Mr. Howarth, of Bridgeman-street Academy, aged 63. 10: Mr. Joseph Hampson, Yew Tree, Over Hulton. He had been guardian for Over Hulton since the formation of the Union in 1838.—April 12: Thomas Johnson Esq., after an illness of only a few days, at his residence, Highfield, Chorley New Road, aged 43 years. The deceased gentleman was hon. sec. of the Subscription Library for nearly ten years, and also a Commissioner of Income Tax for the Bolton district. 23: James Eden, Esq., of Showley Hall, Clayton-le-Dale, aged 78 years. The deceased was the senior partner in the firm of Messrs. Eden and Thwaites, The Meetings Bleachworks, Astley Bridge. He directed his personal estate to be sold in order to found an Orphanage for the reception of infant children who had lost both parents, the trustees being instructed to spend a sum not exceeding £10,000 on the building.—June 3 : Mr. C. Howarth, of Coleman's, Horwich, in the 69th year of his age. 14: Mr. James Cooper, of Dalton-terrace, Bury New Road. He was 63 years of age, and throughout his life he was an unflinching Conservative, and was prominently identified with the Conservative party. 15 : J. S. Turner Greene, Esq., for 25 years judge of the Bolton County Court.17: Mr. Luke McHale,draper, aged 76. He was a prominent Roman Catholic. 21: Benjamin Dobson, Esq., formerly senior partner in the firm of Messrs. Dobson and Barlow, machine makers, Kay-street. The deceased gentleman, who was 51 years of age, died at the Clifton Down Hotel, near Bristol. He was a county magistrate, and for about 18 months an alderman of the borough. 22: C. J. Darbishire, Esq., at Vale Bank, Rivington, in the 77th year of his age. He was the first mayor of Bolton, being elected 1st Dec, 1838, and was on the commission of the peace both for the county and borough. July 1: Mr. Joseph Swift, in the 63rd year of his age, for 25 years master of the Trinity-street Railway Station. 15: At Chorley, aged 46 years, Mr. Josiah Smith Andrews, for many years a reporter on the newspaper press of Bolton.—October 15: Mr. John Stanning, for many years manager of the Halliwell Bleachworks, died at Leyland, near Preston, in his 69th year. 24: Mr. Charles Hopwood, quarrymaster, Harwood, aged 68. He was one of the oldest members of the Board of Guardians, having been first elected on the 29th March, 1844. He was chairman of the Board for eight years, and during that time he laid the foundation stone of the Poor-law Offices in Mawdsley-street. 29: Mr. Benjamin Ashworth, aged 58 years, cemetery registrar, which office he had held since 1856.—November 12: Mr. Henry Baylis, C.E., for some years borough engineer of Bolton, died at Handsworth, near Birmingham. 17: Mr. Samuel Crompton, stationmaster, Southport, killed whilst in the performance of his duty. He was formerly stationmaster at Bolton. 22: Mr. Dan Wood Latham died at his residence, Moses Gate, aged 65 years. He was for a long time a prominent member of the Board of Guardians, and he also for 15 years represented Bradford Ward in the Town Council, first from 1846 to 1852, and then from 1856 to 1865.—December 12: Mr. Alfred J. Heaton, cotton spinner, of the firm of Messrs. C. and A. J. Heaton. 13: John Hargreaves, Esq., in his 74th year, at his residence, Sunning Hill, near Windsor, formerly of Bolton, and for many years in the commission of the peace for the Bolton division of the county.

1875.

JANUARY.—3: Mr. R. Briercliffe's cotton mill, Farnworth, burned down, damages £30,000. 12: Westhoughton and Lostock School Board election ; four Church and four Nonconformist candidates were nominated for the seven seats, and the result was that the former carried all their nominees, whilst of the latter only three were returned:—J. Burgess, 1243; G. Caldwell, 1190; J. Pilkington 1077; J. Stott, 1071. Churchmen; J. Tonge, 648 ; R. Entwistle, 652; G. Green, 651, Nonconformists. The eighth candidate was Mr. R. Lee, who polled 627 votes. 14: J. K. Cross, Esq., M.P., addressed a Liberal meeting in the Temperance Hall. Opening of New Jerusalem Church Schools at Kersley. 21 : Rejection of the new scheme for reconstituting Rivington Grammar School at a large meeting of the ratepayers.

MARCH.—1 : Meeting of ratepayers in the Albert Hall to consider the scheme for making a new line to place Bolton in direct communication with the Midland system. A committee of influential local gentlemen was appointed to carry out a scheme for providing additional railway accommodation for the town. 4: First soiree of the Bolton police force. 26 : Foundation stone of new Primitive Methodist Chapel at Walkden, to cost £4000, and accommodate 750 persons, laid by Miss Hurst, Oakwood, Worsley. Foundation stone of Wesleyan Chapel at New Bury, to cost £1035, and accommodate 350 persons, laid by Mr. J. Hindley. 29: Alderman Green laid the corner stone of St. Matthew's Church, Mountstreet. The contract for the building was £7445, and was taken by Mr. Hugh Yates, Liverpool, the church to seat 1000 persons. 31: Foundation stone of new infant school and lecture hall in connection with St. George's Road Congregational Chapel, laid by Mr. J. Lever. The total cost of the structure including land, was to be £1105. Public recognition of the Rev. C. A. Berry as pastor of St. George's Road Chapel.

APRIL.—1: Grand bazaar in Albert Hall for St. Mark's Church. The amount raised was £1025 16s. 9½d. Opening of the London and North-Western line to Manchester for passenger traffic. 14: Self-acter minders resolved to strike unless the masters restored the 5 per cent., which they took off the wages in the previous autumn; matters looked serious at one time but eventually on the 6th May, the employers gave way, and the threatened strike was averted. 21: J. K. Cross, Esq., M.P., laid the foundation stone of Mawdsley-street Congregational Schools. The estimated cost was £3300, and accommodation was provided for 220 children. 26 : Shocking boiler explosion in the Wheat Sheaf beerhouse, Blackburn-street. The house was completely wrecked and the adjoining premises were much damaged. James Ward, labourer, 50 years old, and Mary Annie Entwistle, 11 months old, daughter of William Entwistle, iron moulder, 76, Blackburn-street, were killed. At the inquest, the jury found that the landlord, William Greenhalgh, had been guilty of great negligence in the management of the boiler which was used for brewing purposes, and that the boiler was a badly conditioned one, but they did not feel justified in the present state of the law in returning a verdict of manslaughter against him.

MAY.—5 : Mr. and Mrs. Pilling appointed governor and matron of the Workhouse. Grand bazaar in the Albert Hall for St. James's Church; £970 was raised. 19 : The 27th L.R.V. went under canvas again for a few days encampment at Lytham. The regiment was under the command of Lieut.-Col. Bailey, and nearly 500 rank and file were on the ground. The corps returned to Bolton on Monday, the 24th May, having on the previous Saturday been inspected by Col. Lyons.

JUNE.—5 : J. McLoughland summoned before the borough Bench for tampering with voting papers at the election of Guardians on the 6th of April, but the cases, 35 in all, were dismissed. 7 : Pike's-lane Board School opened by the Rev. Canon Powell, vicar, chairman of the School Board. The schools were erected from designs of Mr. G. Cunliffe, at a cost of £10,000, and they will accommodate 720 children. 17 : Carpenters and joiners

struck for an advance of 3s. 6d. a week. The majority of the
men left the town and the masters procured others in their
places. On the 7th July the matter was settled by the men
accepting an advance somewhat lower than the sum asked for.
23: New Wesleyan Chapel opened at Bertinshaw. The cost
was £1600, and the accommodation provided was for 346 persons.

JULY—15: The Town Council confirmed the purchase of a
plot of land containing 41,695 square yards, adjoining the Park,
for £11,500, for the purpose of extending the Park and Recreation Ground. 17: Consecration of St. Thomas's Church, Hall-
well, by the Bishop of Manchester; the building cost about
£7000, and was seated for 765 persons. There is an annual endowment of £30 per annum. Messrs. Paley and Austin, Lancaster, were the architects. 18: Last sermons preached in St.
Stephen's Presbyterian Church, Haulgh. 21: The turners and
fitters gave notice to stop work unless their wages were advanced in a week. The dispute was amicably settled without a
strike. Mr. H. Lee laid the memorial stone of a new Congregational Chapel in Derby-street, opposite Pike's View. The estimated cost of the building was £2500, and accommodation was
provided for 450 persons.

AUGUST.—9: Messrs. Hardcastle, Cross and Co.'s new bank
opened for business. 12: Presentation of a purse of £96 10s. to
the Rev. J. C. Nesbitt on his leaving the pastorate of Duke's-
alley Congregational Chapel.

SEPTEMBER.—3: Two children named Elizabeth Derbyshire
and Isaac Jenkinson drowned through falling into the Croal,
which was much swollen in consequence of heavy rain. 9:
Visit of 150 members of the Iron and Steel Institute to Bolton.
They visited the works of Messrs. Walmsley and Son, Hick,
Hargreaves, and Co., the Bolton Iron and Steel Co., and Messrs.
J. Stones and Co., Astley Bridge. 16: Presentation to the
Rev. G. S. Hodges, vicar of St. John's, Wingates, and Mrs.
Hodges, of a silver salver and illuminated address on their
leaving Wingates. 20: Presentation of a gold guard, with
pendant, and purse of gold, of the total value of £30, to the
Rev. A. A. Roffe on his leaving St. Thomas's Church School,
Moses Gate, for St. John's, Wingates. 26: Severe thunderstorm
and gale, by which a large amount of damage was done in
Bolton. 30: End of strike of 240 fitters and turners at Messrs.
Dobson and Barlow's works, Kay-street. The men nine weeks
previous struck for an advance of wages, which was refused,
and they remained out until this day, when the matter was
settled by the firm consenting to give 48 of the men the advance
and the others a portion of it.

OCTOBER.—13: Visit of Cardinal Manning to Bolton, and presentation of an address to him by the Bolton Catholic Association. 17: Raid on Blake's betting-house; capture of 17 men,
all of whom were dismissed by the magistrates at the hearing of
the case, excepting Blake, who was fined £100.

NOVEMBER.—1: Municipal elections. Ten Conservatives and
four Liberals retired, and there were contests in every ward, excepting Church, where the Conservative candidates had a walk
over. Six Conservatives and eight Liberals were returned, but
a petition was presented on the 18th November against the
election of the two Liberal candidates for East Ward, Messrs.
Hamilton and Steele, on the ground of bribery and corruption,

and as they gave notice that they should not oppose it, their seats were declared vacant, and themselves condemned in costs. The election was fixed to take place on December 30th. 5 : The resolution of the Town Council to go to Parliament for powers to extend the borough boundaries so as to take in several of the adjacent townships, rejected by an overwhelming majority at a Town's meeting. 9 : Ald. O. Wolfenden elected Mayor. 12 : Cabinetmakers strike for increase of wages. 17 : Congregational bazaar to raise funds for a chapel in Blackburn Road, opened in the Albert Hall by J. K. Cross, Esq., M.P. The sum raised was £942 18s. 3d. 24 : Rev. B. Crook and Mr. Francis Taylor, cotton spinner, elected members of the School Board without opposition, in the room of the Rev. Canon Carter, deceased, and Mr. H. Lee, resigned. Plans and sections of the Bolton Junctions Railway Company's line to Manchester deposited in the Parliamentary Office.

DEC.—5 : Two youths, named Jas. Higson and Henry Parr, drowned through the breaking of ice on which they were sliding. Jas. Whittle, 36 years of age, farm labourer, found dead from exposure on the Black Heights, Turton. 17 : Great meeting in the Temperance Hall for the repeal of the Indian import duties ; speeches by J. Hick, Esq., M.P., J. K. Cross, Esq., M.P., E. Hardcastle, Esq., M.P., and other gentlemen. 19 : Rev. W. Popplewell, M.A., entered on his duties as incumbent of St. Thomas's Church, Halliwell. Trade generally good.

OBITUARY FOR 1875.

January.—6 : In his 74th year, Mr. Thomas Balshaw, registrar of births and deaths for the Western district of Great Bolton for 40 years. 17 : Mr. John Carney, aged 60, a member of the Town Council from 1855 to 1863.—February. 10 : Aged 59 years, the Rev. Canon Carter, of SS. Peter and Paul's Roman Catholic Church, and senior priest of the town. The deceased gentleman was born at Samlesbury, near Preston, educated at Valladolid, Spain, and at the Roman Catholic college of Ushaw, Durham. After serving in several missions he was appointed to SS. Peter and Paul's in 1847. He was an active member of the Cotton Famine Relief Committee, of the Infirmary Committee, and of the Poor Protection Society. He served on the Board of Guardians for the year 1866-7, and he was elected on the School Board at its formation in 1870, and re-elected in 1873, being second on the list. He was buried in the graveyard attached to St. Joseph's Chapel, Brindle, on Monday, the 15th.—24 : Mr. John Nuttall, at his residence, Rose Hill, Halliwell, in his 80th year. From 1838 to his death, Mr. Nuttall was a member of the Board of Guardians, and also of the Halliwell Local Board from its formation. He was overseer of the township of Halliwell for nearly 30 years, and for many years he was surveyor of highways.—March. 4 : Mr. Matthew Bennett, colliery proprietor Little Hulton, aged 56 years. The deceased gentleman worked in a coal pit until he was 21 years of age, but by rare energy and industry he accumulated a large fortune, and in 1870 became a county magistrate. He was also for a time Chairman of the Little Hulton Local Board. 7 : Inspector Greenhalgh, of the Borough Police Force, aged 32. He entered the force in 1865, and was made inspector in 1872. 9 : Mr. Joseph Farrar, in his 39th year, a frequent contributor to the local press. 13: Mr. Thomas Mason, New Hall Farm, Heaton, in his 65th year. Elected a member of the Board of Guardians in 1858 as representative of Heaton, and continued in office to his death. For upwards of 30 years he was surveyor of highways, collector of Government taxes, and overseer of the poor for Heaton. 14: Mr. Samuel Scowcroft, proprietor of Rosehill and Kersley Collieries, aged 56 years. 24: Mr. John A. Haslam, cotton waste dealer, after an illness of only a few days. He was 46 years of age, and was a member of the Town Council for Bradford Ward from 1864 to 1867, and was also on the Board of Guardians for Little Bolton for 1873-4. April 15: Mr. Alex. Lawson, veterinary surgeon, in his 64th year. 24: Mr. Samuel Wood, of Chapeltown, in his 91st year.—May 3: Mr. George Salt, aged 50 years. Mr. Salt was on the Board of Guardians for Great Bolton, was in the Town Council for Exchange Ward for six years from 1861, and for 13 years he was a member of the Board of Directors of the old Gas Company. 8: Mr. Matthew Gorse, cotton spinner, at the age of 65 years. The deceased served on the Board of Guardians for Little Bolton from 1863 to 1871, with the exception of 1865 and 1866, and he was in the Town Council for East Ward from 1862-5. 17: Peter Ormrod, Esq., banker, and head of the eminent cotton spinning firm of Ormrod and Hardcastle, died at Wyresdale Park, Garstang, in his 80th year. Mr. Ormrod was a Conservative, and always took a warm interest in the welfare of his party. He was one of the representatives of Derby Ward in the Town Council from 1843 to 1846, but he refused to serve again or to accept a seat on the Aldermanic bench, to which he was elected. He was on the commission of the peace, but seldom sat on the bench. His memory will best be preserved by his re-building of the Parish Church, which was completed in June, 1871, at a cost of between £30,000 and £40,000. He was buried on Monday, the 24th May, at Churchtown Church, near Garstang. 26: Mr. J. T. Staton, the well-known Lancashire author, in the 59th year of his age.—June. 7: Mr. Isaac Butler in his 76th year. Mr. R. Beddows, cotton spinner, aged 65 years. 15: Of sunstroke, on board the s.s. Europa, within four days' sail of Bombay, the Rev. John Homer Killick. B.A., aged 34 years, formerly curate of the Bolton Parish Church.—July. 18: Mr. George Clapperton, surgeon, formerly of Moor-lane.—Sept. 17: At the Union Mills, Isle of Man, aged 64 years, Mr. John James Bridson, formerly carrying on business in Bolton. 27: Mr. Thomas Orrell, of Orrell House, cotton spinner, in the 64th year of his age. 30: At Southport, Mr. J. B. Harkness, aged 55 years, one of the oldest master tailors in Bolton.—Oct. 23: Mr. J. S. Scowcroft, aged 75 years, collector of poor-rates in Great Bolton from 1825 to 1847, when he was appointed assistant overseer, which office he held for over 20 years. He was elected a member of the Board of Guardians in 1867, and retained his seat until April, 1875, when he came out as an independent candidate and was defeated.—Nov. 13: At Westhoughton, in his 61st year, Mr. J. R. Scott, ex-superintendent of the Bolton division of the County police; retiring from active duty he was presented with a purse of money.—Dec. 3: Mr. B. Farrar, inland revenue officer, aged 69 years. 28: John Harwood, Esq., J.P., in his 75th year, at Woodsleigh, Heaton. The deceased began business as a baker and flour dealer in 1832, and he was highly successful. In 1859 he built the Woodside cotton mills in Great Lever, in partnership with Mr. Ald. Walmsley, which he carried on to his death, though the partnership was dissolved in 1875. Mr. Harwood first entered the Town Council in 1840, and with an interval of six years he remained in up to 1871, twelve years as Councillor and thirteen as Alderman, being the only one of our municipal representatives who could count a quarter of a century's service. He was Mayor in 1860-61. In politics he was a Liberal, and in religion a Unitarian.

THE CORPORATE DEPARTMENTS INVESTIGATION.

At the monthly meeting of the Town Council, on March 8th, 1875, Mr. Ald. Greenhalgh, in the course of some remarks on the Borough Treasurer's abstract, said it appeared to him that every department of the Corporation was in a disorganised state and required absolute overhauling, and suggested that a meeting of the General Purposes Committee should be called to consider the question. On Wednesday, the 10th, the General Purposes Committee met and appointed the following gentlemen a committee to consider and report on the management and detail working of the various departments of the Corporation :—The Mayor (J. Marsden, Esq.), Aldermen Cannon, Walmsley, Rushton, Greenhalgh, and Wolfenden, Councillors Kevan, Holden, Winder, and Musgrave. They examined into the Gas department first, and in their report they strongly condemned the management, in which they could not recommend the Council to continue its confidence. On the 22nd of April they began to investigate the Borough Treasurer's department, and here again they found grave fault with the management, characterising it as "loose and irregular." The consequence of this was that Mr. T. Halliday was engaged to audit the borough finances for the previous year, and he began on the 17th August. In the course of his audit he required some of the books of Mr. Wrigley, the Waterworks superintendent, but on applying for them, Mr. Wrigley, who was then ill at home, refused to give them up. Measures were resorted to to compel him, but as he still remained obstinate, he was suspended on the 11th September by the Waterworks Committee. On the following Monday, however, the 13th, he sent his keys, and the Mayor (J. Marsden, Esq.) and the Town Clerk (R. G. Hinnell, Esq.) instituted a search in the waterworks office. They found the loose leather wrapper of classification Ledger B, but could not find the book itself, and subsequent inquiries left no doubt that Wrigley had made away with a great number of account books. He was arrested by resolution of the Council on 22nd Sept., and at his examination before the Magistrates, which lasted two days, evidence was produced of defalcations by him amounting to between £5000 and £6000, together with the destruction of the books. Wrigley was committed to the Manchester assizes, and on the 27th Nov. he was tried before Mr. Justice Lush, and being found guilty of having embezzled Corporate moneys he was sentenced to five years' penal servitude. The Borough Treasurer continued

in office for some time, but at the meeting of the
Council, on the 30th of October, he was discharged.
The Council advertised for a successor to Mr. Williamson.
There were 73 applicants, and after considerable deliberation the
Finance Committee recommended the Council to appoint Mr. Geo.
Swainson, of Huddersfield, to the vacant office, which was done
at the meeting on the 15th December. The Waterworks Com-
mittee resolved to divide the duties performed by Wrigley, and
accordingly at their suggestion the Council on the 22nd Decem-
ber appointed Mr. W. Hutchinson indoor, and Mr. R. Swindle-
hurst outdoor, superintendent of the Corporation Waterworks.
The Inquiry Committee subsequently investigated the Streets
Department, including the Borough Surveyor's and the Markets
Department, and reported that the administration of each was
satisfactory.

PARLIAMENTARY REPRESENTATION

OF BOLTON.

(Enfranchised under the Reform Act of 1832; Two Members.)

Population 1831—43,396; 1841—49,747; 1851—61,172; 1861—70,395; 1871—92,655. On March 9, 1868, the Parliamentary boundaries of Bolton were extended by the inclusion of Little Bolton Higher End, Astley Bridge, and part of Halliwell; the population of the Municipal borough at the census of 1871 being 82,854, and of the Parliamentary, as above stated, 92,655. In 1872, the Municipal boundaries were extended by taking in Daubhill, but this part is not included in the Parliamentary borough.

ELECTIONS.

1 : 1832, Dec. 12 and 13 (First Election)—

Lieut.-Col. Robert Torrens (L)	...	627
William Bolling (C)	...	492
John Ashton Yates (L)	...	482
William Eagle (R)	...	107

Torrens and Bolling returned;
1040 electors, 935 voted.

---

2 : 1835, Jan. 7 and 8 (General Election)—

William Bolling (C)	...	633
Peter Ainsworth (L)	...	590
Col. Torrens (L)	...	343

Bolling and Ainsworth returned;
1020 electors, 927 voted.

3 : 1837, July 26 (General Election)—

Peter Ainsworth (L)	...	...	...	615
William Bolling (C)	...	...	...	607
Andrew Knowles (L)	...	...	...	598

Ainsworth and Bolling returned ;
1340 electors, 1079 voted.

4 : 1841, July 4 (General Election)—

Peter Ainsworth (L)	...	...	...	669
Dr. Bowring (L) ...	...	...	...	614
Peter Rothwell (C)	...	...	...	595
William Bolling (C)	...	...	...	441

Ainsworth and Bowring returned ;
1442 electors, 1164 voted.

5 : 1847, July 29 (General Election)—

William Bolling (C)	...	...	...	714
Dr. Bowring (L) ...	...	...	...	652
John Brooks (L) ...	...	...	...	645

Bolling and Bowring returned ;
1531 electors, 1309 voted.

6 : 1848, Sept. 12 (Mr. Bolling having died Aug. 30)—
Stephen Blair (C) returned without opposition,
Joseph Barker, the Chartist candidate, having
been withdrawn.

7 : 1849, Feb. 8 (on Dr. afterwards Sir John Bowring's
appointment to the Consulship of Canton)—

Sir Joshua Walmsley (R)	...	...	631
Thomas Ridgway Bridson (C) ...	...	...	558

Sir Joshua Walmsley returned ;
1457 electors, 1189 voted.

8 : 1852, July 8 (General Election)—

Thomas Barnes (L)	...	...	...	745
Joseph Crook (L)	...	...	...	727
Stephen Blair (C)	...	...	...	717
Peter Ainsworth (L)	...	...	...	346

Barnes and Crook returned ;
1671 electors, 1579 voted.

9 : 1857, March 28 (General Election)—

Capt. William Gray (L C)	...	...	930
Joseph Crook (L)	...	...	895
Thomas Barnes (L)	...	...	832

Gray and Crook returned ;
1933 electors, 1673 voted.

10 : 1859, April 29 (General Election)—

Capt. Gray, L C (second time), and Josep
Crook, L (third time), returned ; no opposition.

11 : 1861, Feb. 11 (Mr. Crook having resigned) Thomas
Barnes (L) returned unopposed.

12 : 1865, July 12 (General Election)—

Lieut.-Col. Gray (C)	...	...	1022
Thomas Barnes (L)	...	...	979
Samuel Pope (L) ...	...	...	864
William Gibb (C)	...	...	727

Gray and Barnes returned ;
2075 electors, 1939 voted.

13 : 1868, Nov. 17 (General Election)—

John Hick (C) ...	...	...	6062
Lieut.-Col. Gray (C)	...	...	5848
Thomas Barnes (L)	...	...	5451
Samuel Pope (L)...	...	...	5436

Hick and Gray returned, the latter for the fourth time ;
No. on register, 12,667.

14: 1874, Feb. 4 (General Election)—

John Hick (C	...	...	...	... 5987
John Kynaston Cross (L)		...	...	5782
Col. Gray (C)	...	...	...	... 5650
James Knowles (L)	...	...	...	5440

Hick and Cross returned, the former for the second time;

No. on register, 12,689; voted, 11,565.

Petition against the return of Mr. Cross tried before Mr. Justice Mellor in the Bolton Town Hall, May 23, 25, 26. 1874. The allegations were bribery, treating, undue influence, and other unlawful acts. The petition was dismissed, but Mr. Cross was ordered to bear his own costs so far as related to the conduct of his personating agents and the sending out of railway passes, the learned Judge being of opinion that those acts were of a character "which might fairly be considered by persons advising the petitioners as likely to void the election." With regard to two alleged cases of bribery, the petitioners were ordered to bear Mr. Cross's costs. Mr. Cross therefore retained his seat.

THE BOLTON
TOWN COUNCIL:

ITS PERSONNEL AND POLITICS,

From the Charter of Incorporation, 1838-76.

1838-9.

THE FIRST ELECTION.

First Council—Elected Friday, Nov. 30, 1838; all Liberals,
the Conservatives looking upon the Charter as invalid,
and consequently taking no part in the elections.

EXCHANGE WARD.

John Hamilton, Hotel-street, tea dealer ....489 votes.
Joseph Skelton, Bowker's-row, gentleman ....491 ,,
Richard Dunderdale, Deansgate, tea dealer ......491 ,,
Davies Rawsthorn, Oxford-street, tobacconist ...488 ,,
Thos. Wallwork, Summerfield, spirit merchant...496 ,,
Henry Macoun, Hotel-street, tailor and draper...487 ,,

BRADFORD WARD.

Chas. J. Darbishire, The Folds, manufacturer...358 votes.
William Naisby, Hotel-street, linen draper.........359 ,,
Jos. Ainsworth, Newport-terrace, cotton spinner 359 ,,
William Wharton, Derby-street, manufacturer...359 ,,
John Rothwell, Deansgate, druggist..................359 ,,
William Leigh, Deansgate, chair maker...........359 ,,

DERBY WARD.

Thomas Tong, Crook-street, yarn agent ....458 votes.
Joshua Crook, Bradford-place, cotton spinner ...458 ,,
Richard Kynaston, Blackburn-street, gentleman 458 ,,
Oliver Nicholson, Blackburn-st., shuttle maker...458 ,,
Jas. Winterbottom, Blackburn-street, gentleman 458 ,,
John Markland, Blackburn-street, pawnbroker...458 ,,

CHURCH WARD.

Robert Heywood, Newport-terrace, Esquire ......277 votes.
James Bayley, Newport-place, cotton manufact. 273 ,,
John Dean, Bradshawgate, gentleman................275 ,,
James Barry, Chorley New-road, flour dealer......273 ,,
John Brown, Churchgate, boot and shoe maker...274 ,,
Jas. Rothwell, Breightmet Hall, cotton spinner 272 ,,

1838-9—(Continued).

EAST WARD.

Andrew Knowles, Bagley Bank, coal merchant....565 votes
James Arrowsmith, Green-street, cotton spinner 563　　"
Thomas Thomasson, High Bank, cotton spinner 570　　"
John Haslam, Mill Hill, manufacturer.............563　　"
John Lomax, Water-street, grocer ....567　　"
John Vickers, Tipping-place, manufacturer ......561　　"

WEST WARD.

Thomas Lee, St. George's-place, gentleman ......297 votes.
Robert Walsh, Park-hill, gentleman ....297　　"
John Yates, Park-hill, pawnbroker ....297　　"
Ed.Nightingale, St.George's-place, manufacturer 290　　"
John Slater, Back-o'th'-bank, bleacher ....296　　"
Charles Ainsworth, Tong, cotton spinner...........296　　"

The number of votes recorded shows that a large proportion of the constituency abstained from taking part in this first election.

1838-9—(Continued).

FIRST MAYOR, ALDERMEN, AND TOWN CLERK.

The first meeting of the Council was held on Saturday, December 1, 1838, in the Little Bolton Town Hall, when the first Aldermen were appointed, as under, all being Liberals :—

Exchange Ward.

Ellis Wood, Bank-street, brazier .... 18 votes.
Thomas Evans, Oxford-street, flour dealer .... 20 ,,

Bradford Ward.

John Cross, Gartside House, manufacturer ...... 28 votes.
*Thos. Mulliner, St. George's-road, accountant... 31 ,,

Derby Ward.

Thomas Gregson, Moor-lane, cotton spinner ...... 35 votes.
John Chapman, Moor-lane, flour dealer .... 25 ,,

Church Ward.

Charles Nuttall, Manchester-road, pawnbroker... 35 votes.
John Mangnall, Spring Cottage, paper manufacturer 33 ,,

East Ward.

Joseph Lum, Bury-street, cotton spinner .... 33 votes.
Edmund Ashworth, The Folds, gentleman .... 30 ,,

West Ward.

Thomas Cullen, West Cottage, cotton spinner ... 35 votes.
Abraham Haigh, Stone Mills, Bridge-street,
    cotton spinner .... 35 ,,

The unsuccessful candidates being :—William Moss, 17 votes; John Goodbrand, 15 ; James Morris, 12 ; and William Blinkhorn, Richard Hulme, Jonathan Settle, and William Goodbrand, 2 each.

Charles James Darbishire, Esq., was then elected as the first Mayor ; and James Winder, Esq., solicitor, who had been one of the most conspicuous advocates of the Charter, was elected as the first Town Clerk of the borough.

* The Aldermen were assigned to the respective wards on the 4th December, but Mr. Mulliner declined to qualify, tendering his resignation " on conscientious grounds," which the Council accepted at a meeting on the 19th December; and Mr. William Moss, of Manchester-road, gentleman, who had stood highest on the list of unsuccessful candidates on the 1st, was elected in his place on the 29th December.

1839-40.

ROBERT HEYWOOD, Esq. (L), MAYOR.

EXCHANGE WARD.

Ald. :—Thomas Evans and Ellis Wood

Coun. : C. J. Darbishire   Coun. : Joseph Skalton
      Henry Macoun   Richd. Dunderdale
      John Hamilton   Davies Rawsthorn

BRADFORD WARD.

Ald. :—William Moss and John Cross.

Coun. : Joseph Lawson   Coun. : Joseph Ainsworth
      Robert Orook   John Rothwell
      William Naisby   William Leigh

DERBY WARD.

Ald. :—Thomas Gregson and John Chapman.

Coun. : Isaac Barrow   Coun. : Oliver Nicholson
      William Green   Richard Kynaston
      Thomas Tong   Jas. Winterbottom

CHURCH WARD.

Ald. :—*Henry Moss and John Mangnall.

Coun. : Joshua Crook   Coun. : John Dean
      James Bayley   James Berry
      R. Heywood (Mayor)   John Brown

* Elected July 22, 1840, in place of Ald. Chas. Nuttall, deceased

EAST WARD.

Ald. :—Joseph Lum and Edmund Ashworth.

Coun. : John Haslam   Coun. : Thomas Thomasson
      Jacob Lomax   Andrew Knowles "
      James Arrowsmith   John Lomax

WEST WARD.

Ald. :—Thomas Cullen and Abraham Haigh.

Coun. : Nathaniel Wilson   Coun. : John Slater
      Robert Haslam   Thomas Lee
      John Yates   Robert Walsh

All Liberals; at the election on the 1st Nov., there was again no contest by the Conservatives, who held that a vote would have been a tacit acknowledgment that the Charter was valid; but amongst Liberals themselves there were one or two contests.

1840-41.

JAMES ARROWSMITH, Esq. (L), MAYOR.

EXCHANGE WARD.

Ald.: Thomas Evans and Ellis Wood.

Coun.: John Hamilton
Davies Rawsthorn
C. J. Darbishire

Coun.: Henry Macoun
Joseph Skelton
Richd. Dunderdale

BRADFORD WARD.

Ald.:—William Moss and John Cross.

Coun.: George Mason
John Harwood
Joseph Lawson

Coun.: Robert Crook
Joseph Ainsworth
John Rothwell

DERBY WARD.

Ald.:—Thomas Gregson and John Chapman.

Coun.: Richard Kynaston
John Ackroyd
Isaac Barrow

Coun.: William Green
Thomas Tong
Oliver Nicholson

CHURCH WARD.

Ald.: Henry Moss and John Mangnall.

Coun.: James Barry
P. R. Arrowsmith
Joshua Crook

Coun.: James Bayley
Robert Heywood
John Dean

EAST WARD.

Ald.:—Joseph Lum and Edmund Ashworth.

Coun.: John Entwistle
John Walsh
John Haslam

Coun.: Jacob Lomax
James Arrowsmith,
Mayor
Thomas Thomasson

WEST WARD.

Ald.:—Thomas Cullen and Abraham Haigh.

Coun.: William Baxter
Peter Lowe
Nathaniel Wilson

Coun.: Robert Haslam
John Yates
John Slater

Charter still the subject of litigation, and Council all
Liberals.

1841-2.

THOMAS CULLEN, Esq. (L), Mayor.

EXCHANGE WARD.

Ald. :—*William Naisby and †Ellis Wood.

Coun. : Joseph Skelton | Coun. : Davies Rawsthorn
Richd. Dunderdale | C. J. Darbishire
John Hamilton | Henry Macoun

* Mr. Naisby, elected November 9, 1841, resigning, Mr. Thomas Kirkman was elected Alderman in his stead on the 10th August, 1842.

† Elected Nov. 9th, 1841, in place of Ald. Thomas Evans resigned.

BRADFORD WARD.

Ald. :—John Cross and William Moss.

Coun. : Joseph Ainsworth | Coun. : John Harwood
Thomas Tong | Joseph Lawson
George Mason | Robert Crook

DERBY WARD.

Ald. : John Chapman and Thomas Gregson.

Coun. : Oliver Nicholson | Coun. : John Ackroyd
John Markland | Isaac Barrow
Richard Kynaston | William Green

CHURCH WARD.

Ald. :—John Mangnall and Henry Moss.

Coun. : Robert Heywood | Coun. : P. R. Arrowsmith.
John Dean | Joshua Crook
James Barry | James Bayley

EAST WARD.

Ald. :—Robert Walsh and *John Vickers.

Coun. : James Arrowsmith | Coun. : John Walsh
Thos. Thomasson | John Haslam
John Entwistle | Jacob Lomax

* Elected Dec. 8, 1841, in place of Ald. Joseph Lum, deceased.

WEST WARD.

Ald. :—Abraham Haigh and Thomas Cullen (Mayor).

Coun. : John Slater | Coun. : Pet. Lowe
John Yates | Nathaniel Wilson
William Baxter | Robert Haslam

All Liberals; the validity of the Charter being still undecided.

1842-3.

ROBERT WALSH, Esq. (L), MAYOR.

EXCHANGE WARD.

Ald.:—Thomas Kirkman (L) and Ellis Wood (L).

Coun.:	John Bolling	C	Coun.:	R. Dunderdale	L
	James Scowcroft	C		John Hamilton	L
	Joseph Skelton	L		Davies Rawsthorn	L

BRADFORD WARD.

Ald.:—John Cross (L) and Henry Moss (L).

Coun.:	Charles Skelton	L	Coun.:	Jos. Ainsworth	L
	Robert Crook	L		George Mason	L
	Thomas Tong	L		John Harwood	L

DERBY WARD.

Ald.:—*John Chapman (L) and Thomas Gregson (L).

Coun.:	T. R. Bridson	C	Coun.:	Oliver Nicholson	L
	John Hardman	C		Rchd. Kynaston	L
	†John Markland	L		‡Thos. Chantler	C

* Mr. Chapman (L) resigning in consequence of ceasing to be qualified, Mr. C. J. Darbishire (L), who had been defeated in the contest for Councillors in Nov. 1841, was elected Alderman in his stead, Feb. 22, 1843.

† Mr. Markland (L) being deceased, Mr. William Haslam (C) was elected in his place Feb 22, 1843.

‡ Three Conservatives elected for Derby Ward on the 2nd Nov., 1842, Mr. Chantler (C) succeeding Mr. Ackroyd (L), deceased.

CHURCH WARD.

Ald.:—John Mangnall (L) and William Moss (L).

Coun.:	Thos. Myerscough	C	Coun.:	John Dean	L
	William Ward	C		James Barry	L
	Robert Haywood	L		P. R. Arrowsmith	L

EAST WARD.

Ald.:—Robert Walsh, Mayor (L), and John Vickers (L)

Coun.:	Stephen Blair	C	Coun.:	Thos. Thomasson	L
	Robert Knowles	C		John Entwistle	L
	Jas. Arrowsmith	L		John Walsh	L

WEST WARD.

Ald.:—Thomas Cullen (L) and Abraham Haigh (L).

Coun.:	Wm. Blinkhorn	L	Coun.:	John Yates	L
	Nathaniel Wilson	L		William Baxter	L
	John Slater	L		Peter Lowe	L

1842-3—(*Continued*).

The long-contested question of the validity of the Charter of Incorporation being at length definitively set at rest by Act of Parliament—the Borough Incorporation Act, which received the Royal Assent on the 12th August, 1842—the Conservatives resolved then to participate in the Municipal government of the town, and the elections thenceforward became more or less of a party character. At the first contest, on the 2nd November, 1842, there being thirteen seats to be filled in consequence of an extraordinary vacancy in Derby Ward, the Conservatives succeeded in returning nine of their party, the Liberals returning four only,—the political character of the Council, no longer wholly of one party, becoming thus 39 Liberals and 9 Conservatives; and another Conservative taking the place of a Liberal by the extraordinary vacancy in Derby Ward in February, 1843, the numbers became further altered to 38 and 10 respectively.

1843-4.

THOMAS GREGSON, Esq. (L), MAYOR.

EXCHANGE WARD

Ald. :—Thomas Kirkman (L) and Ellis Wood (L).

Coun.:	Thos. Parkinson	C	Coun.:	James Scowcroft	C
	James Knowles,			Joseph Skelton	L
	Solicitor,	C		Rich. Dunderdale	L
	John Bolling	C			

BRADFORD WARD.

Ald. :—John Cross (L) and Henry Moss (L).

Coun.:	P. R. Arrowsmith	L	Coun.:	Robert Crook	L
	John Harwood	L		Thomas Tong	L
	Charles Skelton	L		Joseph Ainsworth	L

DERBY WARD.

Ald. :—Thos. Gregson, Mayor (L) and C. J. Darbishire (L).

Coun.:	Peter Ormrod,		Coun.:	John Hardman	C
	Chamber Hall,	C		William Haslam	C
	Thomas Chantler	C		Oliver Nicholson	L
	T. R. Bridson	C			

CHURCH WARD.

Ald.':—John Mangnall (L) and William Moss (L).

Coun.:	Thomas Holmes	C	Coun.:	William Ward	C
	Thomas Green	C		Robert Heywood	L
	Thos. Myerscough	C		John Dean	L

EAST WARD.

Ald. :—Robert Walsh (L) and John Vickers (L).

Coun.:	Robert Burton	C	Coun.:	Robert Knowles	C
	John Hartley	C		Jas. Arrowsmith	L
	Stephen Blair	C		Thos. Thomasson	L

WEST WARD.

Ald. :—Thomas Cullen (L) and Abraham Haigh (L).

Coun.:	George Binks	L	Coun.:	Nathaniel Wilson	L
	Samuel Taylor	L		John Slater	L
	Wm. Blinkhorn	L		John Yates	L

31 Liberals and 17 Conservatives.

1844-5.

JOHN SLATER, Esq. (L), MAYOR.

EXCHANGE WARD.

Ald. :—William Cannon (C) and Ellis Wood (L).

Coun.:			Coun.:	
Roger Hampson	C		James Knowles	C
Edward Bolling	C		John Bolling	C
Thos. Parkinson	C		James Scowcroft	C

BRADFORD WARD.

Ald. :—William Walker (C) and John Cross (L).

Coun.:			Coun.:	
John Hick	C		John Harwood	L
Thomas Tong	L		Charles Skelton	L
P. R. Arrowsmith	L		Robert Crook	L

DERBY WARD.

Ald. :—James Eckersley (C) and C. J. Darbishire (L).

Coun.:			Coun.:	
Peter Rothwell	C		Thomas Chantler	C
William Haslam	C		T. R. Bridson	C
Peter Ormrod	C		*John Hardman	C

* Mr. Hardman (C) being deceased, Mr. John Brimelow (C), the younger, was, on the 25th Feb., 1845, elected in his stead.

CHURCH WARD.

Ald. :—George Piggot (C) and John Mangnall (L).

Coun.:			Coun.:	
John Johnson	C		Thomas Green	C
Johnson Lomax	C		Thos. Myerscough	C
Thomas Holmes	C		William Ward	C

EAST WARD.

Ald. :—George Sharples (C) and Robert Walsh (L).

Coun.:			Coun.:	
Thos. Thomasson	L		John Hartley	C
Joseph Ainsworth	L		Stephen Blair	C
Robert Burton	C		Robert Knowles	C

WEST WARD.

Ald. :—James Greenroyd (C) and *Abraham Haigh (L).

Coun.:			Coun.:	
Jno. Slater, Mayor	L		Samuel Taylor	L
James Knowles,			Wm. Blinkhorn	L
Eagley Bank,	L		Nathaniel Wilson	L
George Binks	L			

* Mr. Haigh (L) being deceased, Mr. Richard Cooper (C) St. George's-terrace, was elected Alderman in his stead, February 28, 1845.

1844-5—(Continued.)

The Council this year presented the unwonted spectacle of a Conservative Council being presided over by a Liberal Mayor, and that Mayor moreover elected by the casting vote of his predecessor. The Conservatives this year for the first time obtained supremacy in our local government. The result of the elections on the 1st November, 1844, when 7 Conservatives and 5 Liberals were returned, left the Liberals a nominal majority of 25 against 23; but as the election of Aldermen on the 9th, following upon the retirement of six Liberal Aldermen, would turn the scale, it was resolved by the Conservatives to contest the appointment to the civic chair. The Liberals nominated Mr. John Slater, and the Conservatives Mr. Stephen Blair. The voting was equal, 24 for each,—Alderman Mangnall, Liberal, voting with the Conservatives. The retiring Mayor (Ald. Gregson) thereupon gave the casting vote to Mr. Slater, who was accordingly elected. The ex-Mayor and five other Liberal Aldermen then left the Council Chamber, having completed their term of office; and the Conservatives being now in actual majority elected six Conservative Aldermen, the position of the parties being thus altered to 29 Conservatives and 19 Liberals. The Council then by 22 votes against 19 removed Mr. Winder from the office of Town Clerk, and by 22 against 10 elected James Kyrke Watkins, Esq., solicitor, as his successor, at a salary of £200 a-year, Mr. Winder's salary having been £300. The Mayor thereupon offered to resign; but the Conservatives unanimously requesting him to retain office, and the Council being thus unanimous in his favour, his Worship consented to retain the chair.

1845-6.

STEPHEN BLAIR, Esq. (C), MAYOR.

EXCHANGE WARD.

Ald. :—William Cannon (C) and Ellis Wood (L).

Coun.: James Scowcroft	C	Coun.: Edward Bolling	C
Thomas Cross	C	James Knowles	C
Roger Hampson	C	Thos. Parkinson	C

BRADFORD WARD.

Ald. :—William Walker (C) and John Cross (L).

Coun.: John Hargreaves, jun.,	C	Coun.: Thomas Tong	L
		P. R. Arrowsmith	L
Joseph Heyes	C	John Harwood	L
John Hick	C		

DERBY WARD.

Ald. :—James Eckersley (C) and C. J. Darbishire (L).

Coun.: T. R. Bridson	C	Coun.: William Haslam	C
Jno. Brimelow, jr.	C	Peter Ormrod	C
Peter Rothwell	C	Thomas Chantler	C

CHURCH WARD.

Ald. :—George Piggot (C) and John Mangnall (L).

Coun.: Thos. Myerscough	C	Coun.: Johnsen Lomax	C
William Ward	C	Thomas Green	C
John Johnson	C	Thomas Holmes	C

EAST WARD.

Ald. :—George Sharples (C) and Robert Walsh (L).

Coun.: Stephen Blair, Mayor	C	Coun.: Joseph Ainsworth	L
		Robert Burton	C
Richd. Crompton	C	John Hartley	C
Thos. Thomasson	L		

WEST WARD.

Ald. :—James Gresnroyd (C) and Richard Cooper (C).

Coun.: Nathnl. Wilsen	L	Coun.: James Knowles	L
James Eden	L	George Binks	L
John Slater	L	Samuel Taylor	L

Conservatives 32, Liberals 16; first Conservative Mayor elected this year, though the Conservatives, as we have seen, were in a majority in the Council from the previous 9th of November.

1846-7.

JAMES SCOWCROFT, Esq. (C), MAYOR.

EXCHANGE WARD.

Ald.:—William Cannon (C) and Ellis Wood (L).

Coun.: James Knowles	C	Coun.: Thomas Cross	C
T. Lever Rushton	C	Roger Hampson	C
James Scowcroft,		Edward Bolling	C
Mayor, C			

BRADFORD WARD.

Ald.:—William Walker (C) and John Cross (L).

Coun.: Alex. Whowell	C	Coun.: Joseph Heyes	C
D. Wood Latham	C	John Hick	C
Jno.Hargreaves,jr.C		Thomas Tong	L

DERBY WARD.

Ald.:—James Eckersley (C) and C. J. Darbishire (L).

Coun.: James Ormrod	C	Coun.: Jno. Brimelow, jr.	C
John Young	C	Peter Rothwell	C
T. R. Bridson	C	William Haslam	C

CHURCH WARD.

Ald.:—George Piggot (C) and John Mangnall (L).

Coun.: Thomas Green	C	Coun.: William Ward	C
John Barrow	C	John Johnson	C
Thos. Myerscough	C	Johnson Lomax	C

EAST WARD.

Ald.:—George Sharples (C) and Robert Walsh (L).

Coun.: John Entwistle	L	Coun.: Richard Crompton	C
Robert Crook	L	Thos. Thomasson	L
Stephen Blair	C	Joseph Ainsworth	L

WEST WARD.

Ald.:—James Greenroyd (C) and Richard Cooper (C).

Coun.: Robert Knowles	C	Coun.: James Eden	L
John Stones	C	John Slater	L
Nathaniel Wilson	L	James Knowles	L

34 Conservatives and 14 Liberals.

1847-8.

THOMAS RIDGWAY BRIDSON, Esq. (C), MAYOR.

EXCHANGE WARD.

Ald. :—Thomas Parkinson (C) and William Cannon (C).

Coun. : Roger Hampson　C
Edward Boiling　C
*James Knowles　C

Coun. : Thos. L. Rushton　C
†John Heaton, stationer,　C
Thomas Cross　C

* Resignation accepted May 10, 1848, and at the same meeting appointed Town Clerk in succession to J. K. Watkins, Esq., resigned.　Mr. Robert Moscrop (C), draper, Deansgate, was on the 13th May elected Councillor in Mr. Knowles's place.
† Elected Nov. 27, 1847, in place of Mr. James Scowcroft (C), elected Alderman.

BRADFORD WARD.

Ald. :—James Hargreaves (C) and William Walker (C).

Coun. : John Hick　C
Wm. H. Wright　C
Alex. Whowell　C

Coun. : D. Wood Latham　C
Jno. Hargreaves, jr.　C
Joseph Hayes　C

DERBY WARD.

Ald. :—*James Scowcroft (C) and James Eckersley (C).

Coun. : Peter Rothwell　C
John Knight　C
James Ormrod　C

Coun. : John Young　C
Thos. R. Bridson, Mayor,　C
John Brimelow, jr.　C

* Elected Nov. 20, 1847, in place of Peter Ormrod, Esq. (C), of Chamber Hall, who had been elected Alderman on the 9th Nov., but declined to accept the office.

CHURCH WARD.

Ald. :—William Gray (C) and George Piggot (C).

Coun. : John Johnson　C
Johnson Lomax　C
*Jonathan Warr　C

Coun. : John Barrow　C
†William Ward　C
Thos. Myerscough　C

* Elected Nov. 2, 1847, in place of Councillor Thomas Green (C), who resigned Oct. 29, 1847, having been appointed manager of the Waterworks.
† Mr. Ward being deceased, Mr. John Scowcroft (C) was on the 24th December, 1847, elected Councillor in his stead.

EAST WARD.

Ald. :—Robert Burton (C) and George Sharples (C).

Coun. : Thos. Thomasson　L
Joseph Ainsworth　L
John Entwistle　L

Coun. : Robert Crook　L
Stephen Blair　C
Richard Crompton　C

WEST WARD.

Ald. :—Richard Cooper (C) and James Greenroyd (C).

Coun. : Thomas Cooksey　C
William Ryder　C
Robert Knowles　C

Coun. : John Stones　C
Nathaniel Wilson　L
James Eden　L

42 Conservatives and 6 Liberals.

1848-9.

THOMAS LEVER RUSHTON, Esq. (C), MAYOR.

EXCHANGE WARD.

Ald.:—Thomas Parkinson (C) and William Cannon (C).

Coun.:			Coun.:	
John Pilkington	C		Edward Bolling	C
Thomas Cross	C		Robert Moscrop	C
Roger Hampson	C		Thos. L. Rushton	
			Mayor,	C

BRADFORD WARD.

Ald.:—James Hargreaves (C) and William Walker (C).

Coun.:			Coun.:	
Joseph Hayes	C		W. H. Wright	C
Thomas Ormrod	C		Alex. Whowell	C
John Hick	C		D. Wood Latham	C

DERBY WARD.

Ald.:—James Scowcroft (C) and James Eckersley (C).

Coun.:			Coun.:	
Thomas Chantler	C		John Knight	C
James Walsh	C		James Ormrod	C
*Peter Rothwell	C		John Young	C

* Mr. Rothwell (C) being deceased, Mr. R. Stockdale (L) was elected to supply the vacancy on the 9th March, 1849.

CHURCH WARD.

Ald.:—William Gray (C) and George Piggot (C).

Coun.:			Coun.:	
Thos. Myerscough	C		Johnson Lomax	C
John Scowcroft	C		Jonathan Warr	C
John Johnson	C		John Barrow	C

EAST WARD.

Ald.:—Robert Burton (C) and *Richard Crompton (C).

Coun.:			Coun.:	
John Lomax	L		Joseph Ainsworth	L
George Binks	L		John Entwistle	L
Thos. Thomasson	L		Robert Crook	L

* Elected Nov. 15, 1848, in place of Ald. Geo. Sharples (C), who had resigned on Nov. 6, in consequence of his removal to Blackpool.

WEST WARD.

Ald.:—Richard Cooper (C) and James Greenroyd (C).

Coun.:			Coun.:	
Geo. Wolstenholme	C		William Ryder	C
Giles Cross	C		Robert Knowles	C
Thomas Cooksey	C		John Stones	C

42 Conservatives and 6 Liberals; but a Liberal taking the place of a Conservative in March, 1849, when Mr. Stockdale was returned unopposed in succession to Mr. Rothwell, deceased, the numbers became 41 and 7.

1849-50.

THOMAS L. RUSHTON, Esq. (C) MAYOR. (Second Year.)

EXCHANGE WARD.

Ald. :—Thomas Parkinson (C) and William Cannon (C).

Coun.: Thos. L. Rushton, Mayor,	C	Coun.: Thomas Cross	C
Robert Moscrop	C	Roger Hampson	C
John Pilkington	C	Edward Bolling	C

BRADFORD WARD.

Ald. :—James Hargreaves (C) and William Walker (C).

Coun.: D. Wood Latham	C	Coun.: Thomas Ormrod	C
T. G. Horridge	C	John Bick	C
Joseph Hayes	C	W. H. Wright	C

DERBY WARD.

Ald. :—James Scowcroft (C) and James Eckersley (C).

Coun.: Rich. Dunderdale	L	Coun.: James Walsh	C
George Dutton	L	Richd. Stockdale	L
Thomas Chantler	C	John Knight	C

CHURCH WARD.

Ald. :—William Gray (C) and George Piggot (C).

Coun.: Jonathan Warr	C	Coun.: John Scowcroft	C
Thomas Barnes,		John Johnson	C
Haslgh,	C	Johnson Lomax	C
Thos. Myerscough	C		

EAST WARD.

Ald. :—Robert Burton (C) and Richard Crompton (C).

Coun.: H. M. Richardson	L	Coun.: George Binks	L
Nathaniel Wilson	L	Thos. Thomasson	L
John Lomax	L	Joseph Ainsworth	L

WEST WARD.

Ald. :—*Richard Cooper (C) and James Greenroyd (C).

Coun.: Robert Knowles	C	Coun.: Giles Cross	C
James Marsden	C	Thos. Cooksey	C
G. Wolstenholme	C	William Ryder	C

* Mr. Cooper being deceased, James Ormrod, Esq. (C), cotton spinner, was elected to supply the vacancy on 5th June, 1850.

39 Conservatives and 9 Liberals.

1850-51.

WILLIAM GRAY, Esq. (C), Mayor.

EXCHANGE WARD.

Ald. :—William Cannon (C) and Thomas Parkinson (C).

Coun.: Roger Hampson C | Coun.: Robert Moscrop C
Charles Johnson C | John Pilkington C
T. L. Rushton C | Thomas Cross C

BRADFORD WARD.

Ald. :—James Hargreaves (C) and William Walker (C).

Coun.: John Hick C | Coun.: T. G. Horridge C
W. H. Wright C | Joseph Heyes C
D. Wood Latham C | Thomas Ormrod C

DERBY WARD.

Ald. :—James Scowcroft (C) and James Eckersley (C).

Coun.: P. R. Arrowsmith L | Coun.: George Dutton L
Rich. Stockdale L | Thos. Chantler C
Rich. Dunderdale L | James Walsh C

CHURCH WARD.

Ald. :—Edward Bolling (C) and William Gray (C), Mayor.

Coun.: John Johnson C | Coun.: Thomas Barnes C
Richd. Mangnall C | Thos. Myerscough C
Jonathan Warr C | John Scowcroft C

EAST WARD.

Ald. :—Robert Burton (C) and Richard Crompton (C).

Coun.: James Haslam L | Coun.: Nathaniel Wilson L
John Knowles C | John Lomax L
H. M. Richardson L | George Binks L

WEST WARD.

Ald. :—James Ormrod (C) and James Greenroyd (C).

Coun.: David Skinner L | Coun.: James Marsden C
Thomas Cooksey C | Geo. Wolstenholme C
Robert Knowles C | Giles Cross C

38 Conservatives and 10 Liberals.

1851-2.

WILLIAM GRAY, Esq. (C), MAYOR. (Second Year.)

EXCHANGE WARD.

Ald. :—William Cannon (C) and Thomas Parkinson (C).

Coun.:			Coun.:	
J. Brown Holden	L		Charles Johnson	C
George Henry	L		Thos. L. Rushton	C
Roger Hampson	C		Robert Moscrop	C

BRADFORD WARD.

Ald. :—William Walker (C) and James Hargreaves (C).

Coun.:			Coun.:	
Wm. Hargreaves	C		Wm. H. Wright	C
Robert Haywood	L		Dan W. Latham	C
John Hick	C		Thos. G. Horridge	C

DERBY WARD.

Ald. :—James Eckersley (C) and James Scowcroft (C).

Coun.:			Coun.:	
William Makant	L		Richard Stockdale	L
James Parkinson	L		Rich. Dunderdale	L
P. R. Arrowsmith	L		George Dutton	L

CHURCH WARD.

Ald. :—Edward Bolling (C) and W. Gray (C) Mayor.

Coun.:			Coun.:	
Thos. Myerscough	C		Richard Mangnall	C
James Greenhalgh	C		Jonathan Warr	C
John Johnson	C		Thomas Barnes	C

EAST WARD.

Ald. : Richard Crompton (C) and Robert Burton (C).

Coun.:			Coun.:	
John Lomax	L		John Knowles	C
Joseph Ainsworth	L		H. M. Richardson	L
James Haslam	L		Nathaniel Wilson	L

WEST WARD.

Ald. :—James Greenroyd (C) and James Ormrod (C).

Coun.:			Coun.:	
John Slater	L		Thomas Cocksey	C
Richd. Wallwork	L		Robert Knowles	C
David Skinner	L		James Marsden	C

31 Conservatives and 17 Liberals.

1852-3.

JOHN STONES, Esq. (C), Mayor.

EXCHANGE WARD.

Ald. :—William Cannon (C) and Thomas Parkinson (C).

Coun.:			Coun.:	
John Harwood	L		George Heary	L
John Orton	L		Roger Hampson	C
J. B. Holden	L		Charles Johnson	C

BRADFORD WARD.

Ald. :—William Walker (C) and James Hargreaves (C).

Coun.:			Coun.:	
Jas. Arrowsmith	L		Robert Heywood	L
John Manchester	L		John Hick	C
Wm. Hargreaves	C		W. H. Wright	C

DERBY WARD.

Ald. :—James Eckersley (C) and James Scowcroft (C).

Coun.:			Coun.:	
George Dutton	L		James Parkinson	L
Rchd. Dunderdale	L		P. R. Arrowsmith	L
William Makant	L		Richard Stockdale	L

CHURCH WARD.

Ald. :—Edward Bolling (C) and William Gray (C).

Coun.:			Coun.:	
William Haslam	C		Jas. Greenhalgh	C
Joseph Cork	C		John Johnson	C
Thos. Myerscough	C		Richard Mangnall	C

EAST WARD.

Ald. :—Richard Crompton (C) and Robert Burton (C).

Coun.:			Coun.:	
T. L. Livesey	L		Joseph Ainsworth	L
H. M. Richardson	L		James Haslam	L
John Lomax	L		John Knowles	C

WEST WARD.

Ald. :—James Greenroyd (C) and James Ormrod (C).

Coun.:			Coun.:	
John Stones, Mayor	C		Rchd. Wallwork	L.
James Marsden	C		David Skinner	L
John Slater	L		Thomas Cocksey	C

27 Conservatives and 21 Liberals.

1853-4.

PETER ROTHWELL ARROWSMITH, Esq. (L), MAYOR.

EXCHANGE WARD.

Ald. :—John Brown (L) and William Cannon (C).

Coun.:			Coun.:		
Thos. Thomasson	L		John Orton		L
P. R. Arrowsmith (Mayor)	L		John B. Holden		L
John Harwood	L		George Henry		L

BRADFORD WARD.

Ald. :—John Cross (L) and William Walker (C).

Coun.:			Coun.:		
James Barlow	L		John Manchester		L
Henry Crook	L		Wm. Hargreaves		C
Jas. Arrowsmith	L		Robert Heywood		L

DERBY WARD.

Ald. :—Thos. W. Heaton (L) and James Eckersley (C).

Coun.:			Coun.:		
Richd. Stockdale	L		Rd. Dunderdale		L
Henry Wilkinson	L		William Makant		L
George Dutton	L		James Parkinson		L

CHURCH WARD.

Ald. :—John Magnall (L) and Edward Bolling (C).

Coun.:			Coun.:		
Richard Harwood	L		Joseph Cork		C
Walter Magnall	L		Thos. Myerscough		C
William Haslam	C		James Greenhalgh		C

EAST WARD.

Ald. :—Nathaniel Wilson (L) and *Richard Crompton (C).

Coun.:			Coun.:		
James Haslam	L		H. M. Richardson		L
Robert Walsh	L		John Lomax		L
Thos. L. Livesey	L		Joseph Ainsworth		L

* Mr. Alderman Crompton (C) being deceased, Councillor Robert Heywood, one of the representatives of Bradford Ward, was elected Alderman to supply the vacancy on 6th Sept., 1854; the vacancy thus occasioned in Bradford Ward not being filled up till the ordinary elections in November.

WEST WARD.

Ald. :—James Knowles (L) and James Greenroyd (C).

Coun.:			Coun.:		
R. M. Haslam	L		James Marsden		C
William Shaw	L		John Slater		L
John Stones	C		Richd. Wallwork		L

1853-4—(*Continued.*)

The Liberals this year—November, 1853—regained their
supremacy in the Council, the Conservatives having been
in a majority from 1844. Twelve Liberal Councillors were
returned on the 1st Nov., 1853, the Conservatives offering
no opposition'; and on the 9th Nov. the position of parties
was still further altered by the retirement of six Conservative Aldermen and the election of six Liberals in their
place; the result being that whereas in the last Council
the Conservatives were in six of a majority, the numbers
being respectively 27 and 21, the Liberals were now in a
majority of 22, the Council at present numbering 35
Liberals against 13 Conservatives. For several years following upon this change, the Conservatives took little part
in the elections; and in such contests as there were for the
three or four succeeding years, they were generally of a
personal rather than a party character, politics being pro-
fessedly out of favour, notwithstanding that the party
element was always predominant whenever there was an
Aldermanic election, not less than in the choice of Mayor.

1854-5.

P. R. ARROWSMITH, Esq. (L), MAYOR. (Second Year.)

EXCHANGE WARD.

Ald. :—John Brown (L) and William Cannon (C).

Coun.: J. B. Holden	L	Coun. : P. R. Arrowsmith	
George Henry	L	(Mayor)	L
Thos. Thomasson	L	John Harwood	L
		John Orton	L

BRADFORD WARD.

Ald. :—John Cross (L) and *James Arrowsmith (L).

Coun.: John Marshall	L	Coun.: Henry Crook	L
J. M. Tait	L	John Manchester	L
James Barlow	L	†James Haddock	L

* Elected Nov. 9, 1854, in place of Ald. William Walker (C), resigned.
† Elected Nov. 18, 1854, on extraordinary vacancy, occasioned by elevation of Councillor James Arrowsmith to Aldermanship.

DERBY WARD.

Ald. :—T. W. Heaton (L) and James Eckersley (C).

Coun.: William Makant	L	Coun.: Henry Wilkinson	L
James Parkinson	L	George Dutton	L
Rchd. Stockdale	L	Rchd. Dunderdale	L

CHURCH WARD.

Ald. :—John Mangnall (L) and Edward Bolling (C).

Coun.: James Bayley	L	Coun.: Walter Mangnall	L
Thos. Scowcroft	L	William Haslam	C
Richard Harwood	L	*Joseph Cork	C

* Mr. Councillor Cork (C) being deceased, Mr. Robert Smalley (L) was elected in his stead, 11th July, 1855.

EAST WARD.

Ald. :—Nathaniel Wilson (L) and Robert Heywood (L).

Coun.: *Joseph Bell	L	Coun.: Robert Walsh	L
Joseph Ainsworth	L	†T. L. Livesey	L
James Haslam	L	H. M. Richardson	L

* Mr. Bell (L) having resigned, Mr. John Vickers (L) was elected to supply the vacancy on 11th July, 1855.
† Mr. Livesey (L) having resigned, Mr. Ellis Bary (L) was elected to the vacancy on the 23rd Feb., 1855.

WEST WARD.

Ald. :—James Knowles (L) and James Greenroyd (C).

Coun.: Rchd. Wallwork	L	Coun.: *William Shaw	L
Rchd. Nightingale	L	John Stones	C
R. M. Haslam	L	James Marsden	C

* Mr. Shaw (L) having resigned, Mr. David Skinner (L) was elected Councillor in his stead, on the 16th May, 1855.

1854-5—*(Continued)*.

At the elections on the 1st Nov., 1854, 12 Liberals were again returned, all unopposed so far as the Conservatives were concerned, but in East Ward there was a contest among the Liberals themselves. As the result of these elections, the Council was now composed of 40 Liberals and 8 Conservatives; and in the following July, a Liberal taking the place of a Conservative Councillor deceased, there was a further disparity of 41 Liberals to 7 Conservatives.

1855-6.

JAMES KNOWLES, Esq. (L), Mayor.

EXCHANGE WARD.

Ald. :—John Brown (L) and William Cannon (C).

Coun.:			Coun.:	
John Harwood	L		George Henry	L.
John Orton	L		Thos. Thomassen	L
John B. Holden	L		P. R. Arrowsmith	L.

BRADFORD WARD.

Ald. :—John Cross (L) and James Arrowsmith (L).

Coun.:			Coun.:	
James Haddock	L		James M. Tait	L.
John Manchester	L		James Barlow	L.
John Marshall	L		Henry Crook	L.

DERBY WARD.

Ald. :—T. W. Heaton (L) and James Eckersley (C).

Coun.:			Coun.:	
William Green	L		James Parkinson	L.
Saml. Hodgkinson			Richard Stockdale	L
William Makant	L		Henry Wilkinson	L.

CHURCH WARD.

Ald. :—John Maugnall (L) and Edward Bolling (C).

Coun.:			Coun.:	
Francis McCormick	L		Thomas Scowcroft	L
Robert Smalley	L		Richard Harwood	L.
James Bayley	L		Walter Mangnall	L.

EAST WARD.

Ald. :—Nathaniel Wilson (L) and Robert Heywood (L).

Coun.:			Coun.:	
Peter Skelton	L		Joseph Ainsworth	L.
H. M. Richardson	L		James Haslam	L
John Vickers	L		Robert Walsh	L.

WEST WARD.

Ald. :—Jas. Knowles (L) Mayor, and Jas. Greenroyd (C).

Coun.:			Coun.:	
James Lomax	L		Rich. Nightingale	L
Robert Haslam	L		R. M. Haslam	L
Richard Wallwork	L		David Skinner	L

44 Liberals and 4 Conservatives; the only Conservatives. in the Council at this time being 4 Aldermen.

1856-7.

JAMES KNOWLES, Esq. (L), MAYOR. (Second Year.)

EXCHANGE WARD.

Ald.:—Fergus Ferguson (L) and John Browr (L).

Coun.:			Coun.:	
Joseph Holden	C		John Orton	L
Thos. Thomasson	L		J. B. Holden	L
John Harwood	L		George Henry	L

BRADFORD WARD.

Ald.:—James Arrowsmith (L) and John Cross (L).

Coun.:			Coun.:	
D. W. Latham	C		John Manchester	L
T. Fildes Johnson	L		John Marshall	L
James Haddock	L		J. M. Tait	L

DERBY WARD.

Ald.:—Richard Stockdale (L) and T. W. Heaton (L).

Coun.:			Coun.:	
Nathan Smedley	C		Saml. Hodgkinson	L
Richard Howarth	L		William Makant	L
William Green	L		James Parkinson	L

CHURCH WARD.

Ald.:—Richard Dunderdale (L) and John Mangnall (L).

Coun.:			Coun.:	
Richard Harwood	L		Robert Smalley	L
William Haslam	C		James Bayley	L
F. Mc.Cormick	L		Thos. Scowcroft	L

EAST WARD.

Ald.:—Robert Heywood (L) and Nathaniel Wilson (L).

Coun.:			Coun.:	
Robert Walsh	L		H. M. Richardson	L
John Slater	L		John Vickers	L
Peter Skelton	L		Joseph Ainsworth	L

WEST WARD.

Ald.:—John Sharples (L) and Jas. Knowles, Mayor, (L).

Coun.:			Coun.:	
R. M. Haslam	L		Robert Haslam	L
David Skinner	L		Richard Wallwork	L
James Lomax	L		Rchd. Nightingale	L

44 Liberals and 4 Conservatives, the latter being returned at the Nov. Elections, 1856, and there being now no Conservative Aldermen in the Council.

1857-8.

WILLIAM MAKANT, Esq. (L), MAYOR.

EXCHANGE WARD.

Ald. :—F. Ferguson (L) and John Brown (L).

Coun. :			Coun. :	
George Henry	L		Thos. Thomasson	L
George Mason	L		John Harwood	L
Joseph Holden	C		John Orton	L

BRADFORD WARD.

Ald. :—James Arrowsmith (L) and John Cross (L).

Coun. :			Coun. :	
John Marshall	L		T. F. Johnson	L
Charles Bowman	L		James Haddock	L
Dan W. Latham	C		John Manchester	L

DERBY WARD.

Ald. :—Richard Stockdale (L) and T. W. Heaton (L).

Coun. :			Coun. :	
W. Makant, Mayor	L		Nathan Smedley	C
Thomas Crook	L		William Green	L
Richard Howarth	L		Saml. Hodgkinson	L

CHURCH WARD.

Ald. :—Richard Dunderdale (L) and *John Mangnall (L)

Coun. :			Coun. :	
Thomas Scowcroft	L		William Haslam	C
Jas. Greenhalgh	C		Robert Smalley	L
Richard Harwood	L		F. McCormick	L

* Ald. Mangnall (L) having resigned, Councillor John Harwood (L) was elected in his stead on the 6th August, 1858; the extraordinary vacancy thus occasioned in Exchange Ward not being filled up till November.

EAST WARD.

Ald. :—Robert Haywood (L) and Nathaniel Wilson (L).

Coun. :			Coun. :	
Jeremiah Marsden	C		John Slater	L
John Cunliffe	L		Peter Skelton	L
Rober Walsh	L		H. M. Richardson	L

WEST WARD.

Ald. :—John Sharples (L) and James Knowles (L).

Coun. :			Coun. :	
James Cottrill	C		David Skinner	L
Joseph Wood	C		James Lomax	L
R. M. Haslam	L		*Robert Haslam	L

* Councillor Haslam ceasing to be qualified, the Council declared the seat vacant on the 14th July, 1858; but the vacancy thus occasioned was not filled up till Nov.

40 Liberals and 8 Conservatives.

1858-9.

WILLIAM MAKANT, Esq. (L), MAYOR. (Second Year.)

EXCHANGE WARD.

Ald. :—Fergus Ferguson (L) and John Brown (L).

Coun.:			Coun.:		
John Orton	L		George Mason	L
J. R. Wolfenden	L		Joseph Holden	C
George Henry	L		Thos. Thomasson	L

BRADFORD WARD.

Ald. :—James Arrowsmith (L) and John Cross (L).

Coun.:			Coun.:		
Dr. Chadwick	C		Charles Bowman	L
Jabez Johnson	L		D. W. Latham	C,
John Marshall	L		T. F. Johnson	L

DERBY WARD.

Ald. :—Richard Stockdale (L) and T. W. Heaton (L).

Coun.:			Coun.:		
John Brandwood	L		Thomas Crook	L
John Nicholson	C		Richard Howarth	L
W. Makant, Mayor	L		Nathan Smedley	C

CHURCH WARD.

Ald. :—Richard Dunderdale (L) and John Harwood (L).

Coun.:			Coun.:		
Alphonso R. Varley	C		James Greenhalgh	C
Robert Smalley	L		Richard Harwood	L
Thos. Scowcroft	L		William Haslam	C

EAST WARD.

Ald. :—Robert Heywood (L) and Nathaniel Wilson (L).

Coun.:			Coun.:		
William Ryder	C		John Cunliffe	L
Thomas Bolton	L		Robert Walsh	L
Jeremiah Marsden	C		John Slater	L

WEST WARD.

Ald. :—John Sharples (L) and James Knowles (L).

Coun.:			Coun.:		
Edward Barlow	C		Joseph Wood	C
Rchd. Wallwork	L		R. M. Haslam	L
James Cottrill	C		David Skinner	L

35 Liberals and 13 Conservatives.

1859-60.

JOHN ORTON, Esq. (L), MAYOR.

EXCHANGE WARD.

Ald. :—John Brown (L) and Fergus Ferguson (L).

Coun. :	Peter Skelton	L	Coun. :	*James Best	C
	James Aspden	L		†James Morris	L
	J. Orton (Mayor)	L		George Mason	L

* Elected Dec. 1, 1859, in place of Councillor J. R. Wolfenden, elected Alderman.

† Elected Dec. 1, 1859, in place of Councillor George Henry, elected Alderman.

BRADFORD WARD.

Ald. :—John Harwood (L) and James Arrowsmith (L).

Coun. :	Dan W. Latham	C	Coun. :	Jabez Johnson	L
	James Marsden	C		John Marshall	L
	Dr. Chadwick	C		Charles Bowman	L

DERBY WARD.

Ald. :—William Makant (L) and Richard Stockdale (L).

Coun. :	Nathan Smedley	C	Coun. :	John Nicholson	C
	*S. Hodgkinson	L		†Richard Howarth	L
	John Brandwood	L		Thomas Creok	L

* Councillor Samuel Hodgkinson (L) being deceased, his nephew, Mr. John Hodgkinson (L), was elected in his stead unopposed on the 1st Nov., 1860.

† Elected Dec. 1, 1859, in place of Councillor Makant, elected Alderman.

CHURCH WARD.

Ald. :—J. R. Wolfenden (L) and Richard Dunderdale (L).

Coun. :	Richard Harwood	L	Coun. :	Robert Smalley	L
	George Fell	C		Thomas Scowcroft	L
	A. R. Varley	C		James Greenhalgh	C

EAST WARD.

Ald. :—*George Henry (L) and Robert Haywood (L).

Coun. :	Thomas Hope	C	Coun. :	Thomas Bolton	L
	James Brearley	C		Jeremiah Marsden	C
	William Ryder	C		John Cunliffe	L

* Elected Nov. 23, 1859 ; Thomas Thomasson, Esq.; elected Alderman on Nov. 9, having refused to accept the office.

WEST WARD.

Ald. :—Robert Walsh (L) and John Sharples (L).

Coun. :	R. M. Haslam	L	Coun. :	Rchd. Wallwork	L
	W. W. Cannon	C		James Cottrill	C
	Edward Barlow	C		*Joseph Wood	C

* Mr. Wood died on the 28th Dec., 1859, but the vacancy was not filled up till the ordinary elections in Nov., 1860.

31 Liberals and 17 Conservatives.

1860-61.

JOHN HARWOOD, Esq. (L), MAYOR.

EXCHANGE WARD.

Ald. :—John Brown (L) and Fergus Ferguson (L).

Coun.: George Mason	L	Coun.: James Aspden	L
Saml. Rawsthorn	C	James Best	C
Peter Skelton	L	John Orton	L

BRADFORD WARD.

Ald. :—John Harwood, Mayor (L), and James Arrowsmith (L).

Coun.: John Marshall	L	Coun.: Dan W. Latham	C
T. H. Arrowsmith	L	Dr. Chadwick	C
James Marsden	C	Jabez Johnson	L

DERBY WARD.

Ald.: William Makant (L) and Richard Stockdale (L).

Coun.: Charles Heaton	L	Coun.: Nathan Smedley	C
Richard Howarth	L	John Brandwood	L
John Hodgkinson	L	John Nicholson	C

CHURCH WARD.

Ald. :—J. R. Wolfenden (L) and Richard Dunderdale (L).

Coun.: F. Mc.Cormick	L	Coun.: George Fell	C
James Greenhalgh	C	A. R. Varley	C
Richard Harwood	L	Robert Smalley	L

EAST WARD.

Ald.:—George Henry (L) and Robert Heywood (L).

Coun : Alfred Ridings	L	Coun.: James Brearley	C
John Bertenshaw	L	William Ryder	C
Thomas Hope	C	Thomas Bolton	L

WEST WARD.

Ald.:—Robert Walsh (L) and John Sharples (L).

Coun.: John Heaton, cotton spinner	L	Coun.: W. W. Cannon	C
James Cottrill	C	Edward Barlow	C
R. M. Haslam	L	Richard Wallwork	L

32 Liberals and 16 Conservatives.

1861-2.

JAMES RAWSTHORNE WOLFENDEN, Esq. (L), MAYOR.

EXCHANGE WARD.

Ald.:—John Brown (L) and Fergus Ferguson (L).

Coun.:			Coun.:	
*James Best	C		Saml. Rawsthorn	C
George Salt	C		Peter Skelton	L
George Mason	L		James Aspden	L

* Elected Dec. 6, 1861, in place of Councillor John Orton (L), elected Alderman.

BRADFORD WARD.

Ald.:—John Harwood (L) and *John Orton (L).

Coun.:			Coun.:	
Jabez Johnson	L		T. H. Arrowsmith	L
†John Openshaw	L		James Marsden	C
John Marshall	L		Dan W. Latham	C

* Elected Nov. 27, 1861, in place of Ald. James Arrowsmith, who had resigned Nov. 20, on leaving Bolton for Southport.

† Elected Nov. 20, 1861, in place of Dr. Chadwick (C), who had been elected unopposed on Nov. 1, but declined to serve, claiming exemption on the ground that he had already served the office of Councillor for three years.

DERBY WARD.

Ald.:—William Makant (L) and Richard Stockdale (L).

Coun.:			Coun.:	
John Brandwood	L		Richard Howarth	L
R. H. Constantine	L		John Hodgkinson	L
Charles Heaton	L		Nathan Smedley	C

CHURCH WARD.

Ald.:—James Rawsthorne Wolfenden (L), Mayor, and Richard Dunderdale (L).

Coun.:			Coun.:	
T. W. Bedhead	L		Jas. Greenhalgh	C
H. M. Richardson	L		Richard Harwood	L
F. McCormick	L		George Fell	C

EAST WARD.

Ald.:—George Henry (L) and Robert Heywood (L).

Coun.:			Coun.:	
Thomas Bolton	L		*Lwrno. Whittaker	C
Roger Haslam	L		Thomas Hope	C
John Bertenshaw	L		James Brearley	C

* Elected Nov. 15, 1861, on extraordinary vacancy occasioned by the death of Councillor Alfred Riding: (L).

WEST WARD.

Ald.:—Robert Walsh (L) and John Sharples (L).

Coun.:			Coun.:	
Edward Barlow	C		*James Cottrill	C
Abraham Pilling	L		Ralph M. Haslam	L
John Heaton	L		Wm. W. Cannon	C

* Councillor Cottrill (C) being deceased, Mr. James Barlow (L) was elected in his stead, September 18, 1861, unopposed.

34 Liberals and 14 Conservatives.

1862-3.

JAMES RAWSTHORNE WOLFENDEN, Esq. (L), MAYOR. (Second Year.)

EXCHANGE WARD.

Ald.:—Fergus Ferguson (L) and John Brown (L).

Coun.:			Coun.:		
William Kenyon	C		George Salt		C
Peter Skelton	L		George Mason		L
James Best	C		Saml. Rawstborn		C

BRADFORD WARD.

Ald.:—John Orton (L) and John Harwood (L).

Coun.:			Coun.:		
Dan W. Latham	C		John Openshaw		L
Thos. Wilkinson	L		John Marshall		L
Jabez Johnson	L		T.H. Arrowsmith		L

DERBY WARD.

Ald.:—Richard Stockdale (L) and William Makant (L).

Coun.:			Coun.:		
John Hodgkinson	L		R. H. Constantine		L
*James Taylor	L		Charles Heaton		L
John Brandwood	L		Richard Howarth		L

* Elected unopposed, Nov. 21, 1862, on extraordinary vacancy caused by the election of Councillor Richard Harwood as Alderman.

CHURCH WARD.

Ald.:—Richard Dunderdale (L) and James Rawsthorne Wolfenden (L) Mayor.

Coun.:			Coun.:		
Rowland Hall	C		H. M. Richardson		L
Richard Stothert	C		F. McCormick		L
T. W. Redhead	L		James Greenhalgh		C

EAST WARD.

Ald.:—Robert Heywood (L) and George Henry (L).

Coun.:			Coun.:		
Thomas Hope	C		Roger Haslam		L
Matthias Gorse	C		John Bertenshaw		L
Thomas Bolton	L		Lwrnc. Whittaker		C

WEST WARD.

Ald.:—Richard Harwood (L) and Robert Walsh (L).

Coun.:			Coun.:		
Ralph M. Haslam	L		Abraham Pilling		L
Wm. W. Cannon	C		John Heaton		L
Edward Barlow	C		James Barlow		L

35 Liberals and 13 Conservatives.

1863-4.

RICHARD HARWOOD, Esq.!(L), MAYOR.

EXCHANGE WARD.

Ald.:—Fergus Ferguson (L) and John Brown (L).

Coun:			Coun.:		
Samuel Rawsthorn	C		Peter Skelton		L
George Mason	L		James Best		C
William Kenyon	C		George Salt		C

BRADFORD WARD.

Ald.:—John Orton (L) and John Harwood (L).

Coun.:			Coun.:		
John Marshall	L		Thos. Wilkinson		L
Ralph Howarth	L		Jabez Johnson		L
Dan W. Latham	C		John Openshaw		L

DERBY WARD.

Ald.:—Richard Stockdale (L) and William Makant (L)

Coun.:			Coun.:		
Charles Heaton	L		James Tayler		L
David Skinner	L		John Brandwood		L
John Hodgkinson	L		R. H. Constantine		L

CHURCH WARD.

Ald.:—Richard Dunderdale (L) and James Rawsthorne Wolfenden (L).

Coun.:			Coun.:		
Peter Foster	C		Richard Stothert		C
Alphonso R. Varley	C		T. W. Redhead		L
Rowland Hall	C		H. M. Richardson		L

EAST WARD.

Ald.:—Robert Heywood (L) and George Henry (L).

Coun.:			Coun.:		
Jeremiah Marsden	C		Matthias Gorse		C
John Thirlwind	L		Thomas Bolton		L
Thomas Hope	C		Roger Haslam		L

WEST WARD.

Ald.:—Richard Harwood (L) Mayor, and Robt. Walsh (L).

Coun.:			Coun.:		
John Heaton	L		Wm. W. Cannon		C
James Barlow	L		Edward Barlow		C
R. M. Haslam	L		Abraham Pilling		L

34 Liberals and 14 Conservatives.

1864-5.

RICHARD STOCKDALE, Esq. (L), MAYOR.

EXCHANGE WARD.

Ald.:—Fergus Ferguson (L) and John Brown (L).

Coun.:			Coun.:	
George Salt	C		George Mason	L
James Best	C		William Kenyon	C
Saml. Rawsthorn	C		Peter Skelton	L

BRADFORD WARD.

Ald.:—John Orton (L) and John Harwood (L).

Coun.:			Coun.:	
John Openshaw	L		Ralph Howarth	L
John A. Haslam	L		Dan W. Latham	C
John Marshall	L		Thos. Wilkinson	L

DERBY WARD.

Ald.:—Richard; Stockdale (L)1 Mayor, and William Makant (L).

Coun.:			Coun.:	
John Brandwood	L		David Skinner	L
John Hiton	L		John Hodgkinson	L
Charles Heaton	L		James Taylor	L

CHURCH WARD.

Ald.:—Richard Dunderdale (L) and James Rawsthorne Wolfenden (L).

Coun.:			Coun.:	
Thos. W. Redhead	L		Alphonso R. Varley	C
H. M. Richardson	L		Rowland Hall	C
Peter Foster	C		Richard Stothert	C

EAST WARD.

Ald.:—Robert Heywood (L) and George Henry (L).

Coun.:			Coun.:	
Samuel Spencer	C		John Thirlwind	L
Abraham Pilling	L		Thomas Hope	C
Jeremiah Marsden	C		Matthias Gorse	C

WEST WARD.

Ald.:—Richard Harwood (L) and Robert Walsh (L).

Coun.:			Coun.:	
Edward Barlow	C		James Barlow	L
*P. R. Arrowsmith	L		R. M. Haslam	L
John Heaton	L		Wm. W. Cannon	C

* Councillor P. R. Arrowsmith having resigned, Mr. Joseph Mellor (L) was elected in his stead on the 20th April, 1865, unopposed.

33 Liberals and 15 Conservatives.

1865-6.

RICHARD STOCKDALE, Esq. (L), MAYOR. (Second Year.)

EXCHANGE WARD.

Ald. :—John Brown (L) and Fergus Ferguson (L).

Coun.:	John Green	C	Coun.:	James Best	C
	Charles Skelton	L		Saml. Hawthorn	C
	George Salt	C		*George Nelson	L

* Elected Nov. 20, 1865, in place of Councillor George Mason, elected Alderman.

BRADFORD WARD.

Ald. :—John Harwood (L) and John Orton (L).

Coun.:	Thos. Wilkinson	L	Coun.:	John A. Haslam	L
	Joseph Brooks	L		John Marshall	L
	John Openshaw	L		Ralph Howarth	L

DERBY WARD.

Ald. :—*William Makant (L) and Richard Stockdale (L) Mayor.

Coun.:	James Taylor	L	Coun.:	John Hilton	L
	Thomas Bromley	L		Charles Heaton	L
	John Brandwood	L		David Skinner	L

* Alderman Makant having resigned, Councillor James Barlow was elected Alderman in his stead, June 18, 1866, the extraordinary vacancy thus occasioned in West Ward not being filled up till the ordinary elections in November.

CHURCH WARD.

Ald. :—J. R. Wolfenden (L) and Richard Dunderdale (L).

Coun.:	John Carney	L	Coun.:	H. M. Richardson	C
	Rowland Hall	C		Peter Foster	C
	T. W. Redhead	L		Alphonso R. Varley	C

EAST WARD.

Ald. :—George Mason (L) and Robert Heywood (L).

Coun.:	George Whittaker	C	Coun.:	Abraham Pilling	L
	Thomas Brown	C		Jeremiah Marsden	C
	Samuel Spencer	C		John Thirlwind	L

WEST WARD.

Ald. :—Peter Skelton (L) and Richard Harwood (L).

Coun.:	R. M. Haslam	L	Coun.:	Joseph Mellor	L
	W. W. Cannon	C		John Heaton	L
	Edward Barlow	C		James Barlow	L

34 Liberals and 14 Conservatives.

1866-7.

FERGUS FERGUSON, Esq. (L), MAYOR.

EXCHANGE WARD.

Ald.:—John Brown (L) and Fergus Ferguson (L), Mayor.

Coun.:			Coun.:	
Saml. Rawsthorn	C		Charles Skelton	L
William Kenyon	C		George Salt	C
John Green	C		James Best	C

BRADFORD WARD.

Ald.:—John Harwood (L) and John Orton (L).

Coun.:			Coun.:	
John Marshall	L		Joseph Brooks	L
Ralph Howarth	L		John Openshaw	L
Thos. Wilkinson	L		John A. Haslam	L

DERBY WARD.

Ald.:—James Barlow (L) and Richard Stockdale (L).

Coun.:			Coun.:	
James Brimelow	L		Thomas Bromley	L
Benj. Whittingham	L		John Brandwood	L
James Taylor	L		John Hiton	L

CHURCH WARD.

Ald.:—J. B. Wolfenden (L) and Richard Dunderdale (L).

Coun.:			Coun.:	
Peter Foster	C		Rowland Hall	C
Robert Stronge	C		Thos. W. Redhead	L
John Carney	L		H. M. Richardson	C

EAST WARD.

Ald.:—George Mason (L) and Robert Heywood (L).

Coun.:			Coun.:	
Jeremiah Marsden	C		Thomas Brown	C
Edward P. Holden	C		Samuel Spencer	C
George Whittaker	C		Abraham Pilling	L

WEST WARD.

Ald.:—Peter Skelton (L) and Richard Harwood (L).

Coun.:			Coun.:	
John Clegg	L		W. W. Cannon	C
James Lomax	L		Edward Barlow	C
Ralph M. Haslam	L		Joseph Mellor	L

32 Liberals and 16 Conservatives.

1867-8.

JAMES BARLOW, Esq. (L), MAYOR.

EXCHANGE WARD.

Ald.:—John Brown (L) and Fergus Ferguson (L).

Coun.:			Coun.:	
Joseph Foy	L		*William Kenyon	C
Chas. Wolfenden	C		John Green	C
Saml. Rawsthorn	C		Charles Skelton	L

* Councillor Kenyon (C) dying October 13th, 1868, Mr. T. L. Rushton (C) was elected in his stead, October 23.

BRADFORD WARD.

Ald.:—John Harwood (L) and John Orton (L).

Coun.:			Coun.:	
Thos. Walmsley	C		*Ralph Howarth	L
William Ramwell	C		Thos. Wilkinson	L
John Marshall	L		Joseph Brooks	L

* Councillor R. Howarth (L) being deceased, Mr. J. K. Cross (L) was elected in his stead on the 31st August, 1868.

DERBY WARD.

Ald:—James Barlow (L), Mayor, and Richard Stockdale (L).

Coun.:			Coun.:	
John Cooper	L		Benj. Whittingham	L
Joseph Robertshaw	L		James Taylor	L
James Brimelow	L		Thomas Bromley	L

CHURCH WARD.

Ald.:—J. R. Wolfenden (L) and Richard Dunderdale (L).

Coun.:			Coun.:	
T. W. Redhead	L		Robert Stronge	C
George E. Gorton	C		John Carney	L
Peter Foster	C		Rowland Hall	C

EAST WARD.

Ald.:—George Mason (L) and *Robert Heywood (L).

Coun.:			Coun.:	
Thomas Lever	C		†John Wood	C
Samuel Spencer	C		George Whittaker	C
Jeremiah Marsden	C		Thomas Brown	C

* Alderman Heywood (L) dying on the 27th October, 1868, Mr. John Thirlwind (L) was elected in his stead on the 21st, to serve until the 9th of the following month.

† Elected Nov. 20, 1867, in place of Councillor E. P. Holden (C), who had met with a fatal accident at his paperworks, Springfield, on November 4th.

WEST WARD.

Ald.:—Peter Skelton (L) and Richard Harwood (L).

Coun.:			Coun.:	
Robert Lord	C		James Lomax	L
H. M. Richardson	C		R. M. Haslam	L
John Clegg	L		W. W. Cannon	C

29 Liberals and 19 Conservatives.

1868-9.

JAMES BARLOW, Esq. (L), MAYOR. (Second Year.)

EXCHANGE WARD.

Ald.:—Fergus Ferguson (L) and John Brown (L).

Coun.:			Coun.:	
James Best	C		Charles Wolfenden	C
John Green	C		Samuel Rawsthorn	C
Joseph Foy	L		Thos. L. Rushton	C

BRADFORD WARD.

Ald.:—Charles Skelton (L) and John Harwood (L).

Coun.			Coun.:	
Thomas Wilkinson	L		William Ramwell	C
Jabez Johnson	L		John Marshall	L
Thomas Walmsley	C		John K. Cross	L

DERBY WARD.

Ald.:—John Thirlwind (L) and James Barlow (L), Mayor.

Coun.:			Coun.:	
Joseph Crook	L		Jos. Robertshaw	L
Thomas Bromley	L		James Brimelow	L
John Cooper	L		Benj. Whittingham	L

CHURCH WARD.

Ald.:—Abraham Pilling (L) and J. R. Wolfenden (L).

Coun.:			Coun.:	
T. M. Hesketh	C		G. E. Gorton	C
Rowland Hall	C		Peter Foster	C
Thos. W. Redhead	L		Robert Strongs	C

EAST WARD.

Ald.:—*James Taylor (L) and George Mason (L).

Coun.:			Coun.:	
William Knowles	C		Samuel Spencer	C
George Whittaker	C		Jeremiah Marsden	C
Thomas Lever	C		John Wood	C

* Alderman James Taylor dying on the 6th August, 1869, Mr. Robert Smalley (L) was elected Alderman in his stead, Aug. 16.

WEST WARD.

Ald.:—Richard Harwood (L) and Peter Skelton (L).

Coun.:			Coun.:	
George Nelson	L		H. M. Richardson	C
R. M. Haslam	L		John Clegg	L
Robert Lord	C		James Lomax	L

28 Liberals and 20 Conservatives.

1869-70.

THOMAS WALMSLEY, Esq. (C), MAYOR.

EXCHANGE WARD.

Ald.:—Fergus Ferguson (L) and John Brown (L).

Coun.:	Thos. L. Rushton	C	Coun.:	John Green	C
	Peter Roscoe	C		Joseph Foy	L
	James Best	C		Chas. Wolfenden	C

BRADFORD WARD.

Ald.:—Charles Skelton (L) and John Harwood (L).

Coun.:	P. C. Marsden	C	Coun.:	Jabez Johnson	L
	Peter Crook	C		Thomas Walmsley	
	Thos. Wilkinson	L		Mayor	C
				William Ramwell	C

DERBY WARD.

Ald.:—John Thirlwind (L) and James Barlow (L).

Coun.:	Henry Sharp	C	Coun.:	Thos. Bromley	L
	Edward Cannon	C		John Cooper	L
	Joseph Crook	L		Joseph Robertshaw	L

CHURCH WARD.

Ald.:—Abraham Pilling (L) and *J. R. Wolfenden (L).

Coun.:	Robert Stronge	C	Coun.:	Rowland Hall	C
	Peter Foster	C		T. W. Redhead	L
	Thos. M. Hesketh	C		†G. E. Gorton	C

* Alderman J. R. Wolfenden (L) having resigned on August 9, 1870, Mr. John Knowles (C) was elected Alderman in his stead on the 19th August.

† Councillor Gorton died August 5, 1870; but the vacancy was not filled up till the ordinary elections in November.

EAST WARD.

Ald.:—Robert Smalley (L) and George Mason (L).

Coun.:	Jeremiah Marsden	C	Coun.:	Geo. Whittaker	C
	John Wood	C		Thomas Lever	C
	William Knowles	C		Samuel Spencer	C

WEST WARD.

Ald.:—Richard Harwood (L) and *Peter Skelton (L).

Coun.:	W. W. Cannon	C	Coun.:	R. M. Haslam	L
	Thomas Hesketh	C		Robert Lord	C
	George Nelson	L		H. M. Richardson	C

* Alderman Peter Skelton (L) dying on April 20, 1870, Mr. Benjamin Dobson (C) was elected in his stead on the 27th April.

1869-70—(Continued).

The second Liberal *régime*, which had lasted from 1858, having come to an end, the Conservatives now entered upon their second tenure of power. Last year the Liberals were in a majority of 28 to 20; but on the 1st November, 1869, after a contest of extraordinary severity, the Conservatives succeeded in winning the whole 12 seats, though no one party had hitherto carried the whole at a contested election; and being then in a majority of 4—26 to 22—in the Council were able once more to elect a Conservative Chief Magistrate, Mr. Walmsley being the first Conservative Mayor since 1858. The Liberals, however, still held all the Aldermen; but two Aldermanic vacancies occurring in the course of the year, and their places being supplied by Conservatives, the Council was then composed of 28 Conservatives and 20 Liberals.

1870-71.

THOMAS WALMSLEY, Esq. (C) MAYOR. (Second Year.)

EXCHANGE WARD.

Ald. :—Fergus Ferguson (L) and John Brown (L).

Coun.:			Coun.:	
Chas. Wolfenden	C		Peter Roscoe	C
Dr. Robert Settle	C		James Best	C
Thos. L. Rushton	C		John Green	C

BRADFORD WARD.

Ald. :—Charles Skelton (L) and John Harwood (L).

Coun.:			Coun.:	
T. Walmsley, Mayor	C		Peter Crook	C
Samuel Crowther	C		Thomas Wilkinson	L
P. C. Marsden	C		Jabez Johnson	L

DERBY WARD.

Ald. :—John Thirlwind (L) and James Barlow (L).

Coun.:			Coun.:	
Christopher Ellis	C		Edward Cannon	C
John Haslam	C		Joseph Crook	L
Henry Sharp	C		Thomas Bromley	L

CHURCH WARD.

Ald. :—Abraham Pilling (L) and John Knowles (C).

Coun.:			Coun.:	
Thos. W. Redhead	L		Peter Foster	C
Thomas Wingfield	C		T. M. Hesketh	C
Robert Strange	C		Rowland Hall	C

EAST WARD.

Ald. :—Robert Smalley (L) and George Mason (L).

Coun.:			Coun.:	
Thomas Lever	C		John Wood	C
T. M. Hewitt	C		William Knowles	C
Jeremiah Marsden	C		George Whittaker	C

WEST WARD.

Ald. :—Richard Harwood (L) and Benjamin Dobson (C).

Coun.:			Coun.:	
T. W. Holden	L		Thomas Hesketh	C
Thos. H. Winder	L		George Nelson	L
W. W. Cannon	C		R. M. Haslam	L

29 Conservatives and 19 Liberals.

1871-2.

WILLIAM WALTER CANNON, Esq. (C), Mayor.

EXCHANGE WARD.

Ald. :—Charles Wolfenden (C) and Fergus Ferguson (L).

Coun.: E. G. Harwood	C	Coun.: *William Nicholson,	
Samuel Griffiths	C	Market-street	C
Dr. Settle	C	Thos. L. Rushton	C
		Peter Roscoe	C

* Elected unopposed, Nov. 20, 1871, in place of Councillor Charles Wolfenden (C), elected Alderman.

BRADFORD WARD.

Ald. :—John Green (C) and Charles Skelton (L).

Coun.: Thomas Walker	C	Coun.: Samuel Crowther	C
W. H. Wright	C	Peter C. Marsden	C
Thomas Walmsley	C	Peter Crook	C

DERBY WARD.

Ald. :—James Greenhalgh (C) and John Thirlwind (L).

Coun.: Arthur L. Briggs	C	Coun.: John Haslam	C
Thomas Bromley	L	Henry Sharp	C
Christopher Ellis	C	Edward Cannon	C

CHURCH WARD.

Ald. :—H. M. Richardson (C) and Abraham Pilling (L).

Coun.: William Flitcroft	L	Coun.: Thomas Wingfield	C
William Hesketh	C	Robert Stronge	C
Thos. W. Redhead	L	*William Smith	C

* Elected Nov. 20, 1871, on extraordinary vacancy caused by Councillor Peter Foster (C) being elected Alderman.

EAST WARD.

Ald. :—Jeremiah Marsden (C) and Robert Smalley (L).

Coun. Thomas Glaister	C	Coun.: Thos. M. Hewitt	C
William Melling	C	John Wood	C
Thomas Lever	C	*John Coop	C

* Elected Nov. 20, 1871, in place of Councillor Jeremiah Marsden (C), elected Alderman.

WEST WARD.

Ald. :—Peter Foster (C) and Richard Harwood (L).

Coun.: Peter Kevan	L	Coun.: Thos. H. Winder	L
William Abbatt	L	W. W. Cannon,	
Thos. W. Holden	L	Mayor	C
		Thomas Hesketh	C

35 Conservatives and 13 Liberals; for the first time since 1850, the Conservatives were able this year (Nov., 1871) to elect six of their own party as Aldermen.

.1872-3.

.W. W. CANNON, Esq. (C), MAYOR.   (Second Year.)

[COUNCIL NOW INCREASED FROM 48 TO 52 MEMBERS
—39 COUNCILLORS AND 13 ALDERMEN—BY THE
ADDITION OF RUMWORTH WARD.]

EXCHANGE WARD.

Ald.:—Charles Wolfenden (C) and Fergus Ferguson (L).

Coun.: Thos. L. Rushton	C	Coun.: Samuel Griffiths	C
Robert Crompton	C	William Nicholson	C
E. G. Harwood	C	Dr. Settle	C

BRADFORD WARD.

Ald.:—John Green (C) and Charles Skelton (L).

Coun.: Peter C. Marsden	C	Coun.: Wm. H. Wright	C
Peter Crook	C	Thomas Walmsley	C
Thomas Walker	C	Samuel Crowther	C

DERBY WARD.

Ald.:—James Greenhalgh (C) and John Thirlwind (L).

Coun.: Edward Cannon	C	Coun.: Thomas Bromley	L
Phineas Hall	C	Christopher Ellis	C
Arthur L. Briggs	C	John Haslam	C

CHURCH WARD.

Ald.:—H. M. Richardson (C) and Abraham Pilling (L).

Coun.: William Smith	C	Coun.: William Hesketh	C
Robert Stronge	C	Thos. W. Redhead	L
William Flitcroft	L	Thomas Wingfield	C

EAST WARD.

Ald.:—Jeremiah Marsden (C) and *Robert Smalley (C).

Coun.: John Wood	C	Coun.: William Melling	C
John Wainwright	C	Thomas Lever	C
Thomas Glaister	C	T. M. Hewitt	C

* Ald. Smalley (L) resigning on the ground of ill-health,
Councillor Thomas Walmsley (C) was elected in his stead,
October 22, 1873.

WEST WARD.

Ald.:—Peter Foster (C) and Richard Harwood (L).

Coun.: Thos. Wilkinson	L	Coun.: William Abbatt	L
John Butler	L	Thos. W. Holden	L
Peter Kevan	L	Thos. H. Winder	L

RUMWORTH WARD.

Ald.:—W. W. Cannon (C), Mayor.

| Coun.: J. R. Simpson | C | Coun.: Robert Taylor | L |
| | | Coun.: Ralph Winward C. | |

1872-3—(Continued).

This year, as observed, the Municipal boundaries were extended, in accordance with the Bolton Corporation Act of 1872, Daubhill and adjacent parts of Rumworth being incorporated within the borough by the name of Rumworth Ward. To this new ward four representatives were assigned,—three Councillors and one Alderman. At the first election, on the 1st November, 1872, there was no contest for Councillors,—two Conservatives and a Liberal being returned by arrangement—Mr. W. W. Cannon (C) to retire in 1875; Mr. Robert Taylor (L) to retire in 1874; and Mr. Ralph Winward (C) to retire in 1873. The Council, on the 9th November, elected Major Hesketh as the Alderman for this Ward,—the numbers being for Major Hesketh (C) 25, and for Mr. Henry Lee (L) 16; but Major Hesketh declining to accept the office, Mr. W. W. Cannon, the senior Councillor for the Ward, was elected Alderman in his stead, unopposed, on the 22nd November, 1872; and the vacancy thus caused in the list of Councillors was filled on the 17th December, by the election of Mr. James Rowland Simpson (C), the seat being contested, and the number of votes for Mr. Simpson being 144, and for Mr. Edward Foster (L) 131.

The political constitution of the Council now was 36 Conservatives and 16 Liberals. The Municipal elections on the 1st November were noticeable as the first in Bolton under the Ballot Act; the result, apart from Rumworth Ward already noted, was the return of ten Conservative and two Liberal Councillors in the six contested Wards,—the 12 retiring Councillors having all been Conservatives.

1873-4.

JEREMIAH MARSDEN, Esq. (C), Mayor.

[WARD BOUNDARIES RE-ARRANGED ; NORTH WARD
CREATED ; AND COUNCIL NOW INCREASED FROM
52 TO 56 MEMBERS—42 COUNCILLORS AND 14
ALDERMEN.]

EXCHANGE WARD.

Ald.—Charles Wolfenden (C) and Fergus Ferguson (L).
Coun.: Ralph Walsh L | Coun.: Robert Crompton C
George Jas. Healy L | E. G. Harwood C
Thos. L. Rushton C | Samuel Griffiths C

BRADFORD WARD.

Ald.:—*P. C. Marsden (C) and Charles Skelton (L).
Coun.: James Fogg C | Coun.: Peter Crook C
Samuel Crowther C | Thomas Walker C
†Charles Norris C | Wm. H. Wright C
* Elected Nov. 14, 1873, in place of Alderman John Green,
resigned.
† Elected unopposed, Nov. 28, 1873, in place of Councillor P.
C. Marsden, elected Alderman.

DERBY WARD.

Ald.:—James Greenhalgh (C) and John Thirlwind (L).
Coun.: Thomas Brown C | Coun.: Phineas Hall C
John Haslam C | Arthur L. Briggs C
Edward Cannon C | Thomas Brearley L

CHURCH WARD.

Ald.:—H. M. Richardson (C) and Abraham Pilling (L).
Coun.: John Barnes C | Coun.: Robert Strouge C
William Sparling C | William Fibcroft L
William Smith C | William Heshoth C

EAST WARD.

Ald.:—Jeremiah Marsden (C) Mayor, and Thomas
Walmsley (C).
Coun.: Alfred Challinor C | Coun.: John Wainwright C
Thomas Lever C | Thomas Glaister C
John Wood C | William Melling C

WEST WARD.

Ald.:—Peter Foster (C) and Richard Harwood (L).
Coun.: Thos. W. Holden L | Coun.: John Butler L
Thos. H. Winder L | Peter Kevan L
Thomas Wilkinson L | William Abbatt L

1873-4 *(Continued).*

NORTH WARD.

Ald. :—Robert Henry Lord (C).
Coun.: Robert Halliwell C | Coun.: Robert Smith   L.
Coun.: John Cooper L

RUMWORTH WARD.

Ald. :—William Walter Cannon (C).
Coun.: Henry Poole   C | Coun.: J. R. Simpson   C.
Coun.: Robert Taylor L

Of the 56 members now composing the Council, 38 were
Conservatives and 18 Liberals. The boundaries of the
wards had been considerably altered this year in accordance with the Bolton Corporation Act of 1872. A portion
of West Ward was constituted into an independent ward,
designated as North Ward; the boundaries of the others
had been re-arranged; while the character of the old
"Metropolitan" or Exchange Ward was completely
altered, politically and socially, by the addition of the
Newtown and adjacent district, inhabited chiefly by Irish
Roman Catholics. To North Ward as to Rumworth Ward
four representatives were assigned,—three Councillors and
one Alderman. The first election for North Ward, on the
1st November, 1873, was so keenly contested on political
grounds that a scrutiny had to take place, which resulted
in the following numbers:—Robert Halliwell (C), 328;
Robert Smith (L), 327; John Cooper (L), George Ryder
(C), and F. Hamilton (L), 306 each; and Major Hesketh
(C), 298. There were thus three all equal for the third
place, and the Presiding Alderman, Mr. Thomas Walmsley (after consulting with the Mayor and Town Clerk),
gave the casting vote, though against his own party, in
favour of Mr. Cooper, Liberal. On the 9th Nov. Mr.
Robert Henry Lord was elected unopposed as the first
Alderman of the new ward.

1874-5.

JEREMIAH MARSDEN, Esq. (C), MAYOR. (Second
Year.)

EXCHANGE WARD.

Ald.:—Thomas Lever Rushton (C) and Charles
Wolfenden (C).

Coun.:			Coun.:		
Thos. W. Redhead	L		George J. Healy	L
F. McCormick	L		*Joseph Brooks	L
Ralph Walsh	L		Robert Crompton	C

* Elected November 18, 1874, in place of Councillor Thomas
Lever Rushton, elected Alderman.

BRADFORD WARD.

Ald.:—Thomas Walmsley (C) and Peter C. Marsden (C).

Coun.:			Coun.:		
Thomas Kay	L		Samuel Crowther	C
William Ramwell	C		Peter Creek	C
James Fogg	C		Charles Norris	C

DERBY WARD.

Ald.:—John Green (C) and James Greenhalgh (C).

Coun.:			Coun.:		
Thomas Bromley	L		John Haslam	C
Matthew Fielding	C		Edward Cannon	C
Thomas Brown	C		*Wm. Nicholson	C

* Elected Nov. 18, 1874, in place of Councillor Phineas Hall,
who had ceased to be qualified.

CHURCH WARD.

Ald.:—Thomas Lever (C) and H. M. Richardson (C).

Coun.:			Coun.:		
William Hesketh	C		William Sparling	C
Thomas Wingfield	C		William Smith	C
John Barnes	C		Robert Stronge	C

EAST WARD.

Ald.:—Thomas Glaister (C) and Jeremiah Marsden,
Mayor (C).

Coun.:			Coun.:		
John Vickers	C		*Joseph Musgrave	C
David Gratrix	C		†John Coop	C
Alfred Challinor	C		John Wainwright	C

* Elected unopposed, Nov. 18, 1874, in place of Councillor
Thomas Lever, elected Alderman.

† Elected Dec. 24, 1874, unopposed, in place of Councillor
John Wood, resigned.

1874-5—*(Continued)*.

WEST WARD.

Ald. :—Ebenezer Green Harwood (C) and Peter Foster (C).

Coun.: Peter Kevan   L | Coun.: Thos. H. Winder   L
James Richardson C | Thos. Wilkinson   L
Thos. W. Holden   L | John Butler   L

RUMWORTH WARD.

Ald. :—William W. Cannon (C).

Coun.: John Miles   C | Coun.: Henry Poole   C
Coun. : James R. Simpson   C

NORTH WARD.

Ald. :—Robert Henry Lord (C).

Coun.: Benj. A. Dobson   C | Coun.: Robert Halliwell   C
Coun. : Robert Smith L.

43 Conservatives and 13 Liberals; the whole 14 Aldermen being now Conservatives.

1875-6.

CHARLES WOLFENDEN, Esq. (C), MAYOR.

EXCHANGE WARD.

Ald :—Thomas Lever Rushton, (C), and Charles
Wolfenden, Mayor (C).

Coun. :			Coun. :	
Joseph Brooks	L		F. McCormick	L
Robt. Dunderdale	L		Ralph Walsh	L
T. W. Redhead	L		George J. Healy	L

BRADFORD WARD.

Ald. :—Thomas Walmsley (C) and Peter C. Marsden (C).

Coun.:			Coun.:	
James Johnson	L		William Ramwell	C
Charles Norris	C		James Fogg	C
Thomas Kay	L		Samuel Crowther	C

DERBY WARD.

Ald. :—John Green (C) and James Greenhalgh (C).

Coun.:			Coun.:	
James Brimelow	L		Matthew Fielding	C
Edward Cannon	C		Thomas Brown	C
Thomas Bromley	L		John Haslam	C

CHURCH WARD.

Ald. : Thomas Lever (C) and H. M. Richardson (C).

Coun.:			Coun. :	
Thomas Fletcher	C		Thos. Wingfield	C
Joseph R. Wood	C		John Barnes	C
William Hesketh	C		William Sparling	C

EAST WARD.

Ald. :—Thomas Glaister (C) and Jeremiah Marsden (C).

Coun.:			Coun. :	
*George Makin	L		David Gratrix	C
*Thos. Wilkinson	L		Joseph Musgrave	C
John Vickers	C		Alfred Challinor	C

* Elected December 30th, 1875, in place of Messrs. Henry
Cunliffe Steele, and Francis Hamilton, Liberals, unseated on
petition. At the contest on the 1st November, the candidates
were Messrs. Steele and Hamilton, Liberals, and Messrs. Richard
Hough and Robert Lawson, Conservatives, the result of the
poll being—Steele, 922; Hamilton, 901; Hough, 854; and Lawson, 853. The two former were consequently declared elected,
and took their seats in the Council accordingly. The Conservatives, however, petitioned the High Court of Justice (Common
Pleas Division) against their return, alleging bribery, treating,
and undue influence, the payment of canvassers, and payment

1875-6—(Continued).

for the conveyance of voters to the poll. Messrs. Hamilton and
Steele thereupon gave formal notice that they did not intend to
oppose the petition, and on the 15th December, Mr. Justice
Brett, sitting in Chambers, declared their election null and void,
their seats vacant, and condemned them to pay costs. The
election to supply the vacancies thus occasioned took place on
the 30th December, when the candidates were—Messrs. George
Makin (L), 977 votes; Thomas Wilkinson (L), 948; Robert
Lawson (C), 944; and Richard Hough (C), 925. Messrs. Makin
and Wilkinson were therefore elected.

WEST WARD.

Ald. :—Ebenezer G. Harwood (C) and Peter Foster (C).

Coun. :			Coun. :	
Joseph C. Haslam	L		James Richardson	C
Joseph Ormrod	L		Thos. W. Holden	L
Peter Kevan	L		Thos. H. Winder	L

NORTH WARD.

Ald. :—Robert Henry Lord (C).

Coun.: Robert Crompton C | Coun. : Benj. A. Dobson C
Coun. : Robert Halliwell C.

RUMWORTH WARD.

Ald. : William Walter Cannen (C).

Coun. : James R. Simpson C | Coun. : John Miles   C
Coun.: Henry Poole (C).

Prior to the elections on the 1st November, 1875, there
were in the Council 43 Conservatives, and 13 Liberals ; of
these, 10 Conservatives and 4 Liberals retired, and there
were returned 8 Liberals and 6 Conservatives, thus leaving
the present constitution of the Council 39 Conservatives
against 17 Liberals, these numbers remaining unaltered by
the subsequent extraordinary elections in East Ward.

Printed in July 2021
by Rotomail Italia S.p.A., Vignate (MI) - Italy